Heal
Your
Inner
Wounds

About the Author

Abby Wynne is a Shamanic Psychotherapist, energy healer, and bestselling author from Ireland. One of the world's leading lights in the field of healing, she teaches people how to connect to their mind, heart, and soul to access their inner wisdom, let go of fear, and become more available for life.

Abby's journey with healing has given her powerful insights on unconditional love and self-compassion. With a background in adult literacy and course design, Abby explains complex concepts in a clear and straightforward manner. She wants to make healing accessible to everyone, so she has offerings available at many different levels of healing, empowering and supporting people to do their inner work with strength and courage. She offers pre-recorded healing sessions and guided healing meditations on her website, and she runs online group healing sessions and programs as well. You can work with Abby one-on-one by appointment.

Connect with Abby's thriving social media community on Facebook, Twitter, and Instagram, or watch one of her videos on Facebook or on her YouTube channel.

Don't forget to visit her website to download your free healing meditations to help you with the work of this book at www .abby-wynne.com/healyourinnerwounds.

HOW TO TRANSFORM
DEEP EMOTIONAL PAIN
INTO *freedom* & *joy*

Heal
Your
Inner
Wounds

ABBY WYNNE

Llewellyn Publications
Woodbury, Minnesota

First Edition
First Printing, 2019

Book design by Samantha Penn
Chakra illustration by Mary Ann Zapalac
Cover design by Ellen Lawson

Llewellyn Publications is a registered trademark of Llewellyn Worldwide Ltd.

Library of Congress Cataloging-in-Publication Data (Pending)
ISBN: 978-0-7387-5707-0

Llewellyn Publications
A Division of Llewellyn Worldwide Ltd.
2143 Wooddale Drive
Woodbury, MN 55125.2989
www.llewellyn.com

Printed in the United States of America

Other Books by Abby Wynne

To my mother and my father, who taught me that even the most seemingly impossible wounds can still be healed.

Contents

Exercises

Disclaimer

Please note that energy healing is not a substitute for medical care. If you have a health problem, always consult a health professional. Any application of the material set forth in the following pages is at the reader's discretion and is his or her sole responsibility.

All the major exercises in the book have been recorded and are available as mp3 files for download. I offer the energy of my audio files as energetic support on your journey. I have created these with transmissions of healing energy imbued in each such that the track does the work for you; all you need to do is listen. Visit www .abby-wynne.com/healyourinnerwounds to download them.

Acknowledgments

I would like to thank my team at Llewellyn Publishing for all their help putting the book together; their appreciation of the value of my content and power of my work is incredibly validating and means a lot to me.

Huge thanks to my love, Ian Wynne, for holding the fort, keeping the flow moving in our house with all our children, looking after me on the days where I was caught in other dimensions, and above all for being my best friend and partner in life.

Thanks to my family for being so generous and supportive of my work—I couldn't do it without you all. Thanks especially to my Megan, Joshua, Mya, and Siân: you are the lights of my life. Big thanks to Regina, Cahal, Donna, and Robert for being in my tag team and helping to keep me in one piece, most of the time!

And thank you to Spirit, my guide, my light. I am of service to you and looking forward to where we will go to next.

Author's Note

I went through a dark period when I was in my twenties; nobody was able help me. I went to all different types of therapists...to no avail. I managed somehow to get through it, and when I was in a better place I decided that I wanted to be the therapist I needed back then.

When I studied psychotherapy, I also did my shamanic training, which awakened a part of me that had been closed off for years. I found words for the things that I already knew, and I learned that we are whole beings, not based solely in our minds held captive by our thoughts.

There is magic in the world—you just have to go to the wounded parts of you to find it buried there. May this book help you rekindle your love of life, ignite the fire in you, and bring the magic back into your world.

Peace Prayer

*I desire neither earthly kingdom, nor even
    freedom from birth and death,*

*I desire only the deliverance from grief for
    all those afflicted by misery.*

*Oh Lord, lead us from the unreal to the real,
    from darkness to light, from death to immortality.*

May there be peace in celestial regions.

May there be peace on earth.

May the waters be appeasing.

*May herbs be wholesome and may trees
    and plants bring peace to all.*

May all beneficent beings bring peace to us.

May thy wisdom spread peace all through the world.

May all things be a source of peace to all, and to me.

Om Shanti, Shanti, Shanti

—Bhagavad Gita XVIII

Introduction

We all experience things we don't enjoy and do our best to move through them so that we can be available for life. However, this doesn't always happen; sometimes our natural response to difficult emotions is to ignore them, bury them deep inside, or lock them away somewhere and throw away the key.

When you heal, part of the work is recognizing that you have done this from time to time. You need to give yourself permission to go deep and do the work of releasing the difficult emotions that you've stored away. It is hard to predict how stuck and solidified these unexperienced emotions may be, and each one is different. When you start to peel away the layers and unravel the threads of however you packed these emotions away, it might hurt.

To let deep emotions and inner wounding heal, you may need to go into a process with it, and it is more than likely that it will hurt. So this book might not be for you right now, and that's perfectly fine. I'm not saying this to lure you into buying it, truly! If you are not in a position right now where you feel stable in your life and able to look at the deep emotional wounds you carry within you, then don't do it.

Healing Work Is Good for You

Deeply buried emotions wrap themselves around organs in your body. Yes, okay, I have no scientific evidence of this, but I don't need any. As you read these words, you can ask yourself if it makes sense. Think about the weight of grief, shame, and guilt, carried over years and years. These emotions really weigh you down, and you carry them around with you everywhere like shopping bags full of items that you don't really need. It gets exhausting carrying around so much weight—psychic weight. Your body's energy flow becomes blocked, the efficiency of your body to heal itself is impaired, you age faster, and you lose your enthusiasm for life.

I've helped thousands of people release deep emotional baggage and heal the deep inner wounding they've been carrying for years. After the process, people say that the color has come back into their lives, they start to experience joy and happiness again, and they even catch themselves waking up in the morning full of brightness and enthusiasm. They feel lighter in themselves, more happiness comes in, more joy shows up in their lives. Know that your inner critic can't say "you should be over this by now" about anything, because healing is not a straightforward, logical process. We are not straightforward, logical beings. And while healing work *is* work, it is healthy and good work. It takes time—there are no rules and there are no "shoulds."

Two Levels of Work
to Improve Your Life

Your day-to-day life is where you live most of the time. If things in your daily life are working well for you and you have good friends, a job you like, and your free time is spent doing things you enjoy yet you feel you've not progressed in your life or there are things that have happened to you that you haven't really looked at, then you can try the deeper work of this book.

If your day-to-day life isn't working well and you find that friends and family take more from you than you get, your job wears you down, and you're not enthusiastic about anything, you really have to address that before you do the work here. Find a copy of my book *How to Be Well,* and do the work there first. When you're in balance and things are settled, you can come back and start to heal your inner wounds.

Your Responsible Adult Self Needs to Be the One Reading This Book

We are not simple two-dimensional beings with needs and wants that are logical. We have needs and wants that at times don't make any sense, longings and behaviors that don't seem to fit, and we need to realize that we're made of Spirit *plus* a body, thoughts *and* emotions mixed together.

If you're here reading this, you already know. You know that there is a part of you that sometimes acts like a child because it *is* a child who didn't have its needs met and thus is frozen in time; as an aspect of you, it shows up from time to time when you're tired and feeling unloved. You have an inner teenager who wants to rebel against conformity, pick a fight with your boss just because, sabotage your relationships, or make you feel like you will never fit in, no matter how hard you try. There is a part of you that feels shame or guilt that wants to hide under the duvet, a part of you that is terrified at the idea of you stepping totally into your power, a part of you that wants to prove to you that you were never worthy...and a part of you that knows that you are.

You need to go into this work with your eyes open, which is what I mean when I ask you to call on your responsible adult self when reading this book. So when you open the chapter "Your Inner Child," it is as if you the adult is reading the chapter with you the child on your own lap so that child-you doesn't get a shock when it sees itself maybe clearly for the first time.

It is possible that you will grow to find my voice supportive and warm or that over time you'll find it harsh and unloving. This will change depending on you, because it's you either hearing or reacting to what I'm saying. Some of the things I'm about to talk about ... well, you might not want to hear them. No matter how traumatic or wonderful you think your life is or was, something here in this book may surprise you, and you may be triggered in a way you don't expect. So go slowly and be gentle with yourself.

Feel Into the Work, Don't Just Think About It

The work I present to you here is for all of the aspects of you: body, mind, and soul. Don't just analyze it and agree or disagree—feel it, step into it, put it on, wear it for a day or two, see what your body says. Ask your heart what it thinks, ask your gut what it says.

We all think we have done our work, but then when we sit with our hearts we find more work that is connected at a deeper level, work we haven't realized we left undone. And then when we go to the stomach with the work, it changes again. This is how I want you to work: feelings are just as important as thoughts. Intuition and instinct are just as important as feelings. Learn how to connect all of them together and become the powerful person that you have the capacity to be.

When I give you a mantra or affirmation as follow-up work, don't just say the mantra in your head; I want you to feel it in your body. Sound out the words, speak them out loud and see if they vibrate with deep leaning for you. Amplify them like an echo in the room and open your heart to the energy of them— then ask yourself to let go of anything that does not believe that mantra 100 percent. This is really stepping into the power of the work offered here to you. You can do it or not do it—there is no middle ground.

How Each Chapter Works

This book is designed in layers so that you can keep coming back and go deeper into it. However, I recommend reading the whole thing through first. That way you get a flavor of what is to come and have the time to prepare and to work through it, if you want. The beauty of working in layers is that the top layer works itself off just by doing the reading. Once you've read the book and feel that top layer releasing itself, come back to the chapter that calls you the most and use the work there to help you excavate those deep layers to find the treasure inside of you.

When you're doing the work, you need to prime yourself for what you intend to do and ask yourself if you have your own permission all the way throughout. If you force something you're not ready for, it could cause more harm than good. You might also want to prepare by creating the space you need to do the exercises as well as prepare your therapist or a friend by letting them know you're going to be doing some inner healing work.

Each chapter sets the scene for the work we are doing with story, context, prose, prayer, or a poem. I will ask you to cast your mind into the work as well so the experience is interactive. With everything I say, notice how it makes you feel and what comes up for you. To really go deep, write it all down—everything you think, feel, and realize as you read. It's an opening into a place where there is wounding, for most people. If not for you, that's okay too, but you wouldn't be here reading this if you had no wounding there.

How the Exercises Work

After I set context and bring you into it with me, I offer exercises to help you that you can choose from. Depending on the context, there could be visualizations, healing work, even pure thinking work. Each part of the work is different to the next. See yourself flowing with change and opening to the wealth of healing that is here for you.

Take some time to create a safe space where you can do the exercises. Make sure you're comfortable: have pillows and blankets around you. You may find your body gets uncomfortable as you release stuck energies, you may also find your temperature changes and you get cold.

Feel free to record yourself speaking the visualization into your phone, and then press Play when you're sitting in meditation. The exercises also work if you hold the book in your hands and read them—layers are cool that way! Play with your process and see what works best for you. I also have helpful downloadable recordings available on my website: www.healyourinnerwounds.com.

Know that you might need a few minutes after the exercise to settle yourself and come back into the day. An exercise may only take ten minutes, but it could take you ten minutes to prepare and another ten minutes to unwind. So don't plan to do these exercises if you don't have the time for them—you can't rush healing.

This Book Is for You

I'm writing this book for lots of people, and I am also writing it for you. It's a framework, a structure, a guideline, but at the end of the day, you're the one who decides what you need. The actual healing work happens when you are still, when you give permission to absorb love and release stuck emotional energies. You might need a week or three to prepare energetically to release something you've been holding on to for twenty years, or you might release it just while reading this book—again, there is no logic here. Take the opportunity to go as deeply as you can so you clear and heal your inner wounds as best as you can. That's the most you can do.

Each chapter ends with a way to integrate the work so that you embody it and so it no longer affects your life in a derogatory way. I find that integration or ceremony work is important. When you honor the work you have done, you validate it so that you truly *know* that you have done it. That way, you really do move on from it. This aspect of you, this part of you that needed healing, this deep wounded part can heal and become part of you instead of being something that holds you back from your life or makes you small or a victim, draining your energy and enthusiasm.

Instead of your inner wounding disempowering you, it becomes your superpower, it becomes your friend. And as you start to heal your inner wounds, to let go of the pain, you create space to let in the joy, light, and beauty that you so deserve.

In Summary

This book may be just the book you need to help you do your deep inner work. Take your time with it and read through each chapter so you know what is going to come up before you jump in. Make sure you have a friend close by or someone you trust in case doing this work brings up difficult emotions. The book is designed to be gentle, but everyone is different. How you react to the work is *your* journey, so go in with your eyes wide open. This book could change your life for the better, if you let it.

This isn't a book designed to heal severe trauma and abuse, though it must be said that the same techniques will work no matter how deep the damage was. So if you were raped, violated, physically abused, or have significant trauma and want to heal that part of you, you *can* do the exercises here, but go lightly in them and look after yourself in them. Bring your severe issues to your therapist because responsible adult-you knows that you're only kidding yourself if you think you can handle it on your own.

Chapter One

Your Inner Child

Aspects of us that do not receive what they need become frozen in time and act out through us from time to time without our awareness. The only way to heal aspects of us that are suffering is to split ourselves apart from them and talk to them directly as if they are an independent being. Once the aspect receives the love and attention it needs, it dissolves into our psyche and becomes embodied as part of us. That's how healing works.

We can pick up all of the pieces of ourselves that were stranded across time and space and love them all, melding them into oneness in this present moment.

In this chapter I will look at how to work with the wounding you may have received as a small child, aged between birth and eleven years old. When we do inner work on our childhood, we can think that we have healed things and move on; however, those parts of us that didn't receive what they needed when they were little live on in us and can act out through us without our awareness. Once you learn how to work with your inner child in an active way, those parts of you get the reassurance they need, and you feel more in control as the grown adult you are.

I sit with my client, Adele, in my healing room on the second floor of a Georgian building in Dublin's city center. We look out the window at the people walking by; from this height they seem very small. "That stranger, there," I say to her, pointing at someone across the road. "Does he deserve to be happy?"

"Of course he does!" she says. "And what about her?" I say, referring to a woman farther down the road.

"Sure she does," says Adele with a sigh, realizing where I'm going with this.

I sit down and face her. "So why can't you let yourself play? Have fun? Do things you enjoy? And really let yourself enjoy them?" I ask.

"I know, I know," she says thoughtfully. "But when I start to do that, I think of Mum who's sick in bed, and my sister who is so stressed out, and I feel like I'm being so selfish."

Adele has come to me because she is having relationship troubles. Her boyfriend says she is too needy, and after breaking up with her and getting back together twice, Adele is terrified that it might happen again... and if it does, it may be the last time. "What has fun and play got to do with my problems with my relationship, anyway?" she asks.

"Well," I say, "if you can play and have fun on your own, if you can become your own source of happiness, you won't need to depend on your boyfriend as your only source. That frees him up, and it frees you up too. It means he can go out and have fun with his friends and it won't upset you so much when he doesn't ask you. It means that you can have fun yourself, anytime you want, without pulling on him to provide that for you."

"I suppose that makes sense," Adele says sheepishly.

"It frees you up from your need for other people besides him to fulfill you," I add, "and it will empower you because you won't feel so disappointed in them when they don't."

"Who would you be if nobody needed you to care for them?" I ask Adele. "And who would you be if you could look after your own needs instead of anticipating everyone else's?" She is silent at this. I continue, "And I'm just wondering, so forgive me if I'm wrong, but do these people really need you to care for them? Or can you see them as adults who are actually able to look after themselves without you? This is a big issue, Adele, and it's not just something you do; many people live this way."

If this resonates with you, it is possible that you feel you have to entangle yourself so deeply in other people's lives in order to feel needed. You justify your actions by knowing that people depend on you, so you are available to them more than you are available to yourself. And when you do something for yourself, just for you, you feel so guilty at not including them that it puts you right off—you just can't fully enjoy it. So you don't do things that make you feel happy on a regular basis; instead you get your joy from fleeting moments when you feel you've accomplished something, because any other time you do something fun, it is always tinged with guilt.

This chapter is for anyone who is the peacemaker in their family, anyone who feels they've not been loved enough as a child because they were the ones minding everyone.

This chapter is also for anyone who looks for the love they didn't get as a child in their current relationships, anyone who finds themselves needing their partner too much and needing their partner to need them back. And if you recognize this pattern of neediness in yourself, do you notice that when you let go of the neediness inside you feel insecure and small in the world, lost, without direction? Does the neediness make you overwhelmed, exhausted, or worn down? Do you lose your temper quickly as a result? All of this is the work of the inner child, the work of feeling valued, of getting all your needs met, learning need versus want, play versus work. These patterns live on in us as adults, and they can be mastered and healed.

Inner child work isn't a new thing, yet it is complicated. Different aspects of your own your inner child may act up, throw a temper tantrum, or shut you down completely depending on what is going on in your life…and you might not realize it is happening.

I see us as amalgamations of all the different aspects of ourselves, all the personas and all the ages we have been over the whole of our lives. So the responsible adult part of you is here with me, reading this chapter, while your inner child is possibly sulking somewhere waiting for an opportunity to jump out at you and say, "This isn't true!" or "I told you so!" If you can start to see yourself as both adult and child, you will begin to notice when you slip into the child and be able to take control and claim yourself as the adult again. For this to truly be useful, you need to accept that this is just something that is, and then you can find more patience to deal with the child inside of you. Use this work as an opportunity to step up to the person you are becoming, to be the adult who looks after you and all the parts of you, instead of letting the child take over completely—the child who wants to throw a tantrum and wreck everything.

When a baby or child does not receive enough love, the individual as an adult can feel like they are not good enough, that something is wrong with them, and that they have to over-achieve or be totally of service to their partner in order to receive the love they crave. In this chapter I will be looking at how you can learn to receive love, how to break the patterns of overextending yourself in order to receive love, and how to let yourself enjoy your life without guilt.

Your inner child could use this work as an excuse to fall apart. But are you going to allow that to happen? Know that it doesn't have to be like that. If you feel right now that your abandoned child part is stronger than your responsible adult part, then you will have to get help. This is important work, so don't choose not to do it; instead, find someone to support you as you work. There are wonderful therapists out there who can help you process your inner child work or simply be there to witness you as you work through this book. See the appendix for help as to how to choose someone to support you in your healing process.

You're the responsible adult here, and you have a say in how you handle your healing process. So let your inner child come out for healing, and then gently let go of the child part and claim your adulthood again, knowing that your inner child feels seen and heard and has received the love it has been craving. Doing so will let you feel more at ease with yourself in your life.

Know that you can come back and do these exercises as many times as you need, so go gently. Taking on too much all at once can be overwhelming. We need to heal our inner child by taking baby steps.

Healing Your Inner Child

Most people go through the world looking for the love, validation, and approval they may have never received from their parents. When the adult doesn't get what their inner child is looking for, the inner child can take over and the adult can revert to child-like behavior. This can be anything from temper tantrums (and in an adult this can be quite scary!) that push the loved one away, to sulking in the corner feeling sorry for themselves, wondering why their loved one has left them again. It usually turns into a struggle of self-criticism, blame, and anger directed inward.

"It's my fault nobody loves me because I am unlovable." If this resonates with you, the first and best thing you can do is to learn how to accept love, validation, and approval from yourself. This is very difficult and can take a long time, so please do the exercises here but don't expect them to take hold right away. It will take time to grow into a new way of being. You will need to be patient with yourself, just as you would be patient with a toddler.

Here I work with the Abandoned Child, the Caregiver Child, and the Wounded Child, the most common types of inner children we all carry around with us in some form or other. The way I work is fluid and abstract, yet practical and transformational. Read each section before trying the exercises so you are prepared for the work ahead; take time to think about them before you do them if needed. Proper preparation for healing is 80 percent of the work.

The Abandoned Child:
Learning How to Give and Receive Love

I had a client who came to me because she found her severe dislike of herself was leaking out and onto her children. She couldn't stand to be in a room with her six-year-old son because his joy irritated her so much that she wanted to shout or, worse, lash out at him. This seems severe and extreme (and yes, it was), but it's a prime example of transference: what we feel about ourselves transfers itself to the people around us.

When we went deeper into the work, my client admitted that she never felt close to either of her parents and didn't remember feeling loved and secure at any stage of her childhood. It wasn't that she was jealous and spiteful and withholding love from her son; she didn't know how to receive love. When she would hold her son, he would give his love to her and she would shut down. Being shut down over long periods of time led to her pushing him away and being small and angry at herself because she was starving for affection too.

I want you to learn from this extreme example of how being unable to receive love can affect a person's ability to give love. And then I want you to see if you can apply this to yourself. In fact, I want you to see if you can apply some part of everything in this book to yourself, as inner wounds can be so deep that you just don't recognize them when they show up in your behavior. This woman who could not receive love could not look at herself in a mirror either. She could not tolerate her own reflection. It might not be as bad for you, but one of the qualities of an abandoned child is that they do not like or love themselves at all because they decided at one point or another that because they were abandoned, they must be unlovable.

I believe the biggest problem we have is that we neglect to go to the universal source of unconditional love for love; instead we go to other people. Most people have flawed personalities and just do not know how to love another person unconditionally. This creates a cycle or a chain where unsatisfied people who are looking for unconditional love only receive conditional love.

The way we get conditional love is to fill the conditions for that love, and who better than a child to be molded around conditions? Children will do anything to be loved, so they change their behavioral patterns in order to receive conditional love, and their patterning continues as they grow into adults.

As adults we meet other adults from different families who come with different conditioning, different patterning. I believe the main cause of unhappiness within relationships is the friction created between adults who have subconscious conditions for love but do not get those conditions met by their partner. Bringing those patterns and conditions into the conscious mind can help smooth relationships a lot, but until we realize that people have their limitations and cannot fill us with what it is we really crave, we will always be fighting with each other.

Here is your opportunity to break this chain in you and learn how to receive a source of unconditional love. Know that you can receive this at *any time*. There is no limit to the supply. There is as much of it here as you would ever want, and it will never be denied to you.

Then with this in mind, you no longer need to go to a person to give you what you need. You no longer need to set conditions to receive unconditional love. You, in turn, can release people from your pattern of need because you will no longer need them to fulfill you. You can let them be free to be completely who they are, flaws and all, allowing you freedom to be who you are too. Wonderful!

Exercise

Journaling

Get a notebook and pen. Ask yourself the following questions and then write down the answers. Really go deep with this and take as long as you need. If it's too much then take a break and come back to it. The more accurate your answers are and the more thought you put into this part of the work, the deeper the healing and transformation will be.

- Are you allowed to feel love without fear?
- What are your fears around feeling totally and completely loved for who you are?
- Are these fears real ones, or have you created them?

If deep down you believe that love will be taken away from you once you allow yourself to receive it, know that the only one who has the power to shut it all down is you.

- Would you do that to yourself?
- What do you need for yourself so that you don't shut down?
- Where in your body do you get tight and tense when you imagine yourself receiving love?

If you are feeling resistance to this exercise, ask yourself:

• What is the worst that can happen if I do this work?

Be prepared to not be able to feel anything at all because you may have become so hardened when it comes to life that you're really not ready for this. If this is the case, you might need an emotional release before you can allow yourself to feel love.

• Are you okay when it comes to crying? What can you do to cry?

Sometimes just knowing that a good cry is what you need can start the process for you. You can put a boundary around the crying before you begin, give yourself permission to do it, and know that becoming emotional has a beginning, middle, and an end—it will not cause you to fall apart and go into a crisis.

Receiving Love as a Responsible Adult

The next exercise is an introduction to what it feels like to receive unconditional love. It could be difficult to do this at first, so take it in your own time, at your own pace. Set a timer for this so that you feel safe knowing there is a beginning, middle, and end to this exercise. Five minutes is a good time to start with, and you can then build it up to ten, fifteen, or even twenty minutes at a time. Just know that you might need a few minutes after the exercise to settle yourself and come back into the day. Don't plan to do these exercises if you don't have the time for it—you can't rush healing.

It would be beneficial to set up a quiet space for yourself where you can do all the exercises to come. You don't need fancy lighting, candles, or incense, but if you like that stuff then go for it! As long as you feel safe and you won't be disturbed, you will be able to go as deep into the work as you are able to. If you feel you didn't go deep enough, know that each day you're different, so try it again another day and perhaps you'll get the breakthrough you're looking for.

Exercise

Receiving Unconditional Love

Breathe and relax. Tune in to the rhythms of your body, your breathing, and the speed of your thoughts (imagine a hamster running in a wheel: the speed of the wheel maps to the speed of your thoughts—can you slow it down just by paying it attention?).

Connect to your heartbeat, and give yourself permission to slow down all these cycles, all these rhythms. What do you need to do in order to allow yourself to slow down right now? Give it to yourself.

Speak out loud, "I give myself permission to receive unconditional love." What changes in your body? Do you feel excited or nervous? Sometimes it can be difficult to tell the difference.

Now breathe and relax and feel your feet flat on the ground, or if you can't place them on the ground, make sure you feel supported by wherever you are sitting or lying.

Imagine a beautiful glowing pink ball of light just above your head, like your own personal sun. This light shines at the vibration of love; it's soft and gentle and matches how your body is feeling today. You don't have to believe in anything or need to really know how this works—just try it, go wholeheartedly into it, and see what it feels like to let go of your hesitations and let the light in.

As you breathe and relax, imagine the ball of light is connecting into your energy field. Breathe and receive this light into your personal space. Stay here for as long as you feel comfortable; allow your body to relax more and more as you receive the light.

There are a few things you can try in order to feel the light more strongly. Here are a few ideas; see if you can come up with more for yourself.

- Imagine that as you go through life you have placed layers of protection around you that stop you from feeling love. As you get comfortable with the light, see if you can peel away a layer of protection (like an onion skin or banana peel) and let more light seep into you. See how many layers you can remove in a sitting. Come back, do it again, and learn how many layers you put back on just by being in your life. This is a normal thing; don't be upset if you feel you're getting nowhere for a while—you're on your path.

- Imagine that the beautiful pink light sinks slowly into your energy field and changes you into a pink light. Imagine your skin, your bones, your blood, all dissolving away until you become a ball of light too. Make sure that when you're ready to come back into the room after doing this that you bring awareness into the whole of your body before you jump up and get back into your daily activities.

- Let the ball of light activate a ball of light inside your heart center (at your breastbone) so that you have a ball of light over your head and a smaller one in your heart. As you breathe in and out, relax and allow the ball of light in your heart center to expand slowly, until it becomes the same size as the ball of light above your head. Let the balls of light "speak" to each other, changing color, vibration, and frequency. Notice how your body feels as you do this. Again, take time to come back into the room before you go about your daily activities.

Your Responsible Adult Can Give Love to Your Abandoned Child

As you get a handle on the many aspects that make you who you are, you may begin to notice when you slip back into your abandoned inner child part who craves love, demands attention, and feels abandoned and rejected. These are the times when you need to stop, slow down, and then step gently but firmly back into your responsible adult self.

If you've been practicing receiving unconditional love, you will have the strength and the ability to now love your abandoned child part until they feel safe, wanted, and cherished again. It's so freeing. The first few times you do this exercise, make sure you have free time and a safe space so you can go gently into it. Once you're used to it, you might find yourself able to do this exercise more quickly in the moment if you find yourself slipping back into child mode. You can use it to pull yourself out of a potentially damaging situation, if you catch it in time.

The more often you do this exercise, the easier it gets. As with any child, know that offering love one time only isn't going to be enough. Even after years of working with my own inner child, I still find myself doing this for myself at times. It's also interesting to note that the childlike part of you in need of love in the moment can be of any age, depending on the circumstances. Whatever the age of the child you sense, know that it is the part of you hurting the most in that moment. Once you no longer hesitate to open your heart to yourself, the pain eases and there's no more drama.

Exercise

Giving Love to Your Abandoned Inner Child

Setting the Scene

Imagine a safe space in nature. With my clients, I find that a big, wide open meadow with lots of wildflowers (and possibly a playground somewhere in it) works really well, but go with whatever landscape comes up for you.

There is a beautiful blanket on the ground with a picnic basket on it that has food your inner child will adore.

Imagine you are sitting on the blanket, resting your eyes, breathing softly, and waiting for your inner child to come visit you. Feel the blanket. What is it made of? The more details that come to life in your mind, the more real the work will feel.

Let your inner child come. They will show up in this image and be the age at which you need the most healing in this moment, right now.

Baby Work

If the child is a baby, you will need to baby it. It's a bit different from a child who understands language.

It might just appear in your arms, or there may be a crib that appears with the baby in it. How do you feel when you look at yourself as a baby? Is the baby crying? How do you feel about picking it up? Can you? Try it.

Hold the baby like you would hold any baby, but know that this is you, holding you as a baby. You might want to rock back and forth holding the baby until you get used to it. If this is as far as you're able to go, that's okay; come back and do more another time.

See if can you sit in a peaceful silence with your inner baby child. You can offer them a bottle from the basket or a piece of crusty bread to suck on if they're teething. See their big face looking up at you, smiling at you, offering you pure love. Notice how it is you who having trouble with the love here, not your baby child.

Now try the exercise from earlier, the pink ball of light. Do it however you find it comfortable, letting that love into you. See your heart activating, and come into balance with the baby in your arms.

Offer the love to the baby by opening your heart to it. Notice how the baby's heart also opens when yours does. Stay here for a while and come into balance with this.

As your heart starts to glow, the baby's heart also glows. Feel the connection between you and your inner baby child. See that baby's face smiling at you, so proud of you. You allow yourself to be proud of that baby too.

Speak to baby if you want to, and know that there is deep healing happening here. Allow emotion to well up in you, cry it out, breathe through it. You are not your emotions—you're just experiencing a release that is enabling you to receive and give love to this precious piece of you.

Now stand up when you're ready, and notice there is a crib beside you. Place the baby gently in the crib, and sit back down on the blanket beside the crib, with your heart open.

Take as long as you need to allow the images to dissolve away, and bring your awareness back into the room.

Know that this particular exercise is very difficult, and you will need space afterward to embody what you did. Don't get the phone or talk to anyone else for a good twenty minutes after this work so that you can truly embody the richness of what you have just done. Get a cuppa, go for a walk, or just sit and look out the window for a while. Well done.

Child Work

Your inner child will approach you as you sit on the blanket as soon as they are ready. Sense where they are and allow yourself to make a connection. Notice how you feel when you see your inner child—what's *your* reaction?

Are they sheepish, or do they want to talk to you? Do they rush over for a hug, or are they angry at you? Allow the images to unfold like a movie. Don't let your brain take over, just be with the landscape.

You might want to lay out a delicious tea from your picnic basket and invite your inner child to come eat with you, or your inner child may want you to come explore the landscape with them—if so, go! Know that the lightness that you bring to this work will enable you to let go of the emotional pain that much easier.

Talk to your inner child—ask them how they are, ask what they need from you. Listen to them—they represent an aspect of your inner wisdom that you've been ignoring.

Know that you are the responsible adult and that it is your job to look after your inner child now. Have you been doing that? Apologize to your inner child, let them know that you're still learning how to look after them properly. Ask what you can do better next time. If it's unreasonable, then explain why you can't do what the child wants you to do.

Let the child know that they are truly, deeply loved. If it helps, imagine this is just a child and not *you* as a child. However, your subconscious mind knows that it is you, so this part might be a little difficult at first.

If the child wants to come sit with you, play beside you, climb up onto your lap, or give you a hug, be with that pink ball of light first. Let go of those layers of protection—know that this is you loving a part of you, unconditionally. Know that there is nothing threatening here, that you are the adult, and your inner child needs love. This is the love you crave. Open to your child, sit with them, open to that pink ball of light and love, feel your heart opening, and tell your inner child that you're so sorry they didn't get what they needed. Tell them that you're here now and you're learning how to love them better. Tell them that you *do* love them, that you're proud of them, that you are both on the same team.

There may be emotional release. This is big work. Allow it to come, whether it's from the child or from you. There is only love here. Know that there is only love here in this landscape.

When the embrace releases, your inner child may want to play. Perhaps there is a playground nearby that you can go to, or they may want to collect wildflowers, sing or dance, or even swim in a pond or a river. Enjoy the images; this is the freedom, respect, and space of love that you long for in your everyday reality. So experience the freedom, the love, and the joy with your inner child right here, right now.

Know that you can come back anytime, that your inner child will come to you here as you develop trust and commitment in your relationship. Know that as you work with them, they will be less likely to sabotage your behavior and take over your life because they now know they will be seen and heard, respected and loved. And that's all they wanted in the first place.

Come back to the blanket and sit. Allow the images to slowly dissolve away. Bring your awareness back to your daily life. You will need some time to integrate what you've done; it is big work and different every time. Give yourself the space you gave to your inner child to rest and come back into balance.

Bringing It All Together

These are mighty powerful exercises. They may be all the work you need to do to heal your inner child self. Doing them once won't solve it, however, and doing the releasing work won't be as powerful if you don't do the preparation work. But you know all of this.

The more time you spend connecting to your responsible adult self, the better you know yourself and the quicker you will catch yourself slipping back into abandoned child energies. Notice what feels different when you're acting out, as even your language may be different. Once you start to catch yourself doing it, you can flip quickly in your mind to the image where you hold your child and tell them that you will never abandon them—not ever, no matter what. Say exactly the words you wanted to hear when you were that small. If it helps, you can say them to yourself too, as the adult: "I will never abandon myself." You could even put context around it depending on the situation: "Even if (insert name here) walks away from me, I will never abandon myself again." It is very reassuring.

You might need to remind your inner child several times a day that you are here to look after you; remember that abandonment is a fundamental breach of trust, and it can take years to build up that trust again. You're doing this with you, so nobody will let you down if you commit to the work. As you relax more and trust yourself more, the intensity of the amount of work you need to feel safe and loved will dissipate over time. You will be able to love freely and have closer intimacy in your relationship with yourself and everyone around you. You will be less needy, less clingy, and less demanding as you learn to meet your own needs. Well done.

The Caregiver Child: Learning How to Say No

I had a birthday party when I was five years old, and someone said to me, "Your party was the best party I ever went to!" I was so thrilled when they said that, I felt like I was glowing. So the very next birthday party I went to, I said very loudly as I was leaving, "This was the best birthday party I ever went to!" in the hopes that the birthday girl would hear me. I felt happy that I said something that would make her feel as happy as I did. The next birthday party

I went to, I said it again, but it didn't resonate as much with me because I wasn't really believing it was the best party, and I didn't really feel the joy around saying it, yet I said it because I wanted to make that birthday girl happy too. I don't remember if I said it a third or fourth time because I knew at that point that it wasn't the truth, it wasn't the best party ever. As adults we do this same thing, and when we lie and make statements similar to "Your party is the best one I've ever been to" just to please someone when we don't believe it, it actually eats away a little bit of our soul. Being inauthentic to ourselves and others drains our power and life force, and it's time to stop doing that.

The birthday party example explains how you might feel when you say yes to babysitting your friend's children for the sixth time this month (when you really wanted to go to that movie), or when you say yes to a family dinner that you know will upset you and cause you to feel drained and exhausted for days afterwards. But saying no is something that you as a caregiver child would have never even thought of as an option; you just did what had to be done at the time no matter what the cost was to your soul. And now as an adult, the pattern is ingrained and you have great trouble saying no to things, primarily because you don't really have your own permission to do that.

Take some time to work on this. It might take a while, in fact, as you peel back the layers you have put down around this issue. You might not even be aware that you're doing it. Let's start with a journaling exercise.

Exercise

Journaling

Get a notebook and write the answers to these questions. Be honest with yourself—it doesn't pay you not to be. You can always burn the answers afterwards.

- Are you aware when you say yes to things that you really would prefer to say no to, or do you realize it after you've already said yes?

- In the last week, how many times did you say yes to something that you didn't want to say yes to? Is there a pattern to the things that you say yes to? If so, what is it? Write down all the reasons why you needed to say no instead of yes. Look back at the last week and imagine yourself saying no to a few of those things. How does it feel?

- In the last month, how many times did you say yes to something that you didn't want to say yes to? How did you feel when you did those things? How did you feel after you did those things? Do the exercises from above again, only apply them to a month instead of a week.

- What was the biggest thing this year that you said yes to that you really didn't want to do? What was the result for you of doing that? Do you think you would do this again? What was the learning? Do you see your pattern more clearly now after doing this exercise? If you could go back in time to the you that said yes, what would you say that would have helped you realize what you were doing and say no instead?

- When was the last time you said no to something? Did you find it easy to do? Do you have the words handy for saying no? Write down five different ways you could say no to something based on what you have said yes to over the past year.

- Do you feel guilty when you say no? As the responsible adult in you becomes more aware of the inner caregiver child who says yes, what could you do to look after both your inner child *and* your responsible adult self in these situations?

This is a big exercise and can possibly cause you some upset once you realize your pattern. However, what needs to heal must be revealed, so take as long as you need to take and be as honest as you can. Finding the truth can reveal so much more about you that you may not be aware of.

Releasing Your Responsible Adult from the Caregiver Child Pattern

There are two parts to this: the first is for your conscious mind, the second for your subconscious mind.

Exercise

Consciously Saying No in a Healthy Way

You might need to take some time to figure out different ways that you can say no. Think of when someone said no to you; if it hurt you maybe that's why you have trouble with it. Bring that to the deep inner work we do next.

Now come up with some powerful but loving ways to say no and write them down. If it helps, think of a real situation that you wanted to say no to but couldn't. Speak them out loud to try them out. How firm are you being? Just think of a door—are you shutting the door completely with what you are saying, or are you leaving it slightly open? Are you giving someone permission to kick open your door? Make sure you know what you want before you say it. Be authentic; don't say you wish you could say yes but you can't, if you don't.

Here are some examples to get you started:

- "I just don't have the energy to take on anything else right now."
- "I'm not able to do this thing you've asked of me."
- "I don't have the time available to give it the energy that it deserves."

Now think about the following:

- If you heard someone saying these things to you, would you respect them? Then why wouldn't they respect you when *you* say it? What is the deep hidden belief in you that warrants a lack of respect in your direction?

Remember, you can always buy yourself more time to make a decision. You never have to say yes to anything immediately unless it's truly an emergency.

If you are having trouble with this exercise, my book *How to Be Well* can help you take your power back from people, places, and things, as well as help you center and ground yourself, and stand firm in what you're believing and saying. It's a great complement to the work that we are doing here, and certainly worth a look.

Subconscious Release Work

This is an exercise for which you need to be relaxed, comfortable, and somewhere you feel safe. Don't pressure or force yourself, and don't rush it. Just be at ease as best as you can with who you are and where you are right now. Take a reading on where you are before you begin. Say out loud, "I am allowed to say no" and see how it feels to say it. Do you mean it? Fifty percent? One-hundred percent? Just test how it feels to say it, see where you are with it. Then when you're ready, do this exercise.

Exercise

Clearing What's in the Way of Your Ability to Say No

Breathe, and slow down your thoughts and your body. Take a good five or even ten minutes to do this. With every breath, notice how you slow down even more. The longer you spend doing this the deeper the work will go.

Allow your body to feel the hurt and pain it feels around being said no to in the past. Feel that *no* resonating through you, and know that it was your child who felt it, not the adult.

Visualize a space in nature where you feel safe, and allow yourself to go there in your mind. Hear the noises beneath your feet. Notice what the weather is doing. Spend some time bringing yourself there as strongly as you can.

As you walk around exploring, find a safe space where your inner child can come and meet you. See yourself appear, at whatever age you felt that *no*, that rejection, and open your heart. Let the healing light come in.

Talk to your inner child if you're able to. Hold them and reassure them that they are good enough just as they are. Remind them that a no isn't a no to *them*, it's a no to a thing. Tell your inner child how great they are and smile at them. Let them know that they grew up, they made it, and look—here you are! If you feel there is deeper work to be done here, you can go into the Healing an Aspect of Yourself meditation on my website that can help hold you for as long as you need while the wounding opens, unravels, and releases.

Thank your inner child for showing up, tell them that we are allowed to say no too, and you're going to learn how to do that so that you have more energy to have fun and enjoy your life.

Say thank you and end in an embrace. Let the child disappear off into the distance, then dissolve away the images and bring your awareness back into the room with your body.

Open your eyes. Feel released from the hurt of saying no all through your body now.

Feel your feet connected strongly to the ground and say to yourself, "I am allowed to say no!"

How does that feel? Stronger than when it did at the start of this exercise? Are you able to hold the energy of "I am allowed to say no"? I think you notice the difference already!

Bringing It All Together

To make this work stick with you over time, you need to consolidate it. Listen to your inner wisdom the next time someone asks you to do something. Silently repeat the key phrase "I am allowed to say no" to yourself. You can then ask yourself, "Do I really want to do this? Do I have the energy to do this?" before jumping right in and saying yes.

Take time every day for a week to go back into the image of the landscape and work with your inner child. It doesn't have to be long, and you don't have to have an agenda; just show up there and say hello. Ask yourself how you're doing, if your inner child needs anything from you. Deep down, that part of you just wants to be loved and so says yes to everything in fear of being rejected. As you accept all the parts of yourself, this aspect of you will come into ease with life, and you will care less about what others think and more about what you need to do for *you* in your own life.

You won't become mean-hearted or selfish; you are simply increasing the quality of your life and the quality of your presence, and choosing what things you want to invest your life force in more deliberately. I call this being responsible for yourself, which is a far cry from being selfish. Selfishness is taking more than you need to the detriment of others, whereas here you're taking what you need, which you may have never done before. The lesson is about learning the difference between what you want and what you need; the ability to give yourself what you need is good self-care, not selfishness. So say yes to the things that call to you and feel right, and *do* go out of your way for people when they need your help … and also start noticing when saying yes feels wrong on the inside, and honor that feeling by saying no.

The Wounded Child:
Learning How to Have Fun without Guilt

When I'm processing my inner work, healing a wound, or making sense of something that has happened in my life, I find that I need to play. I have learned that time in play helps me consolidate my inner work as it gives me space, helps me ground, and increases my tolerance for life because I have given myself the space I need. Play has an important purpose for me, and that really eases the pressure I would have put on myself if I didn't understand or thought I was just "wasting time." My clients need play too, and so do you. I play computer games, color pictures, and play with my dog and my children. I also love to read for fun, particularly novels with magic, magicians, and dragons! What do you like to do for fun?

This part of the work is lighter than the other parts we have looked at, yet it is just as important. When you take downtime through play, you become stronger in your sense of who you are, more at ease with the world, and your overall happiness levels increase. You could see it as further consolidation work combining the "receiving love" part from earlier in the chapter, along with the "saying no" part we have just done. Now we are learning how to say yes to fun, and that brings with it much relief and joy.

Most of us are wounded children who have grown up. What would the world be like if nobody celebrated or allowed themselves to enjoy their lives? Awful! So see yourself as stepping into a new kind of energy becoming a role model as you allow yourself to be someone who can have fun without feeling guilty about it. If this idea brings up resistance, that's where you start.

Exercise

Journaling

Get your notebook and pen and answer the following questions.

- In reality, who would actually resent you having fun? Can you make a list? Can you go into this and discern what their reasoning may be? Is it reasonable? Or is this all in your mind?

- What about your idea of wasting time? What should you be doing instead? Is this a pressure you are putting on yourself? Now that I've explained the role of play in consolidating inner work and increasing levels of happiness in your life, can you see the value in it? What has changed for you? What ideas can you let go of now?

- When was the last time you really had fun? What were the circumstances around that? Why did you let yourself absorb the joy around you?

- What do you currently do for fun? What have you never done that you would like to try? What do you feel right now is more important to you than having fun? Is this the truth?

Like the saying goes, nobody wishes they had worked harder when they're on their death bed. And the idea of the bucket list as a list of things to do before we die is, I think, often used as an excuse for not having simple and accessible fun in our daily lives. Make your life overall one you enjoy by having more fun in a more manageable way more often.

Let's be clear—having fun the way I am talking about here does not include meeting people on social occasions. Meeting your friends may often be fun, but you need to value your alone-time fun too. And if the people you meet pull on you, put you in situations where you are finding yourself saying yes when you should say no, or you find yourself emotionally drained after meeting them, become more aware of it and be more discerning when deciding what to do for yourself.

Breaking the Pattern of Guilt around Having Fun

Sometimes the only way to break a pattern is to just break it! Settle on an activity that you enjoy—it could be crafting, artwork, or a sport you do for the sheer fun of it. Or choose something new and sign up for classes or watch some lessons on YouTube. My children and I spent months working on Loom Band creations out of colored bits of elastic bands. We watched plenty of tutorials for free on YouTube and had so much fun creating, wearing, and sharing our designs.

After you spend time doing the exercises earlier in this chapter, you may be more familiar with your inner child, so having a dialogue with them is much easier. It's time for a conversation with your inner child about having fun.

Exercise

Talking with Your Inner Child

Go to your landscape, and know that the landscape could change as you are changing; you are always in flow and in flux.

Ask to meet your inner child to chat about having fun. Breathe and wait, slow down, and allow one of the many aspects of you to show up in your mind's eye. You may be surprised at who appears!

Say hello to them, sit and talk, ask how they are. See if your inner child gives their approval for the activity you have chosen—perhaps there was something you used to do and love that you've forgotten about.

Let your inner child know that you're doing this as the adult now, that they might need to teach you how to have fun, and would that be okay with them? Ask them if they would come with you to this new activity and remind you how much fun you love to have.

Always end a meeting with your inner child with an embrace and connection to love, opening your heart and feeling the warmth between you both.

Connect to gratitude as you let the images dissolve away, knowing that you have your full permission to start being more present in your life for love, joy, and fun.

One of my clients used to love making clothes for her dolls. After she did this exercise, she remembered everything about it and she started doing it again with her grandchildren, who adored the new creations. So let your inner child unlock the creativity in you that you may have forgotten about while you were caught up in the seriousness of your life.

Again, this work may take some time for you to integrate. If there's an aspect of you that is still getting in the way of your fun and play, it could be time to do some inner teenager work, which will be covered in the next chapter.

Know that when your inner child is happy, this makes you, the responsible adult, happy too.

Feeling Seen and Heard in the World

The work you have done in this chapter has built up your sense of self, security, and presence in the world. To build trust with yourself at this deep level fosters hope, relaxes you around love, and gives you a certainty and a voice in your relationships around setting good and healthy boundaries.

Here's a final exercise for you to do so that you no longer feel like you're a child in the world, so you feel big and strong in your connection to your life and the people around you.

Exercise

Consolidation Work

Take some time in a safe space to relax and consciously bring your awareness into your body. Try a body scan, a centering exercise, or a body-reconnection exercise; any of these would be helpful here. I have some on my website if you need extra help. The longer you spend slowing down and connecting to your body, the more relaxed you will feel, and the more profound the result from the rest of this work.

Feel your feet on the ground and imagine them sinking through the floor, through the building if you're inside, through foundations, cement, rock, stone, and soil, connecting into the soft, welcoming earth.

Go down as deeply as you feel you can with your imagination. Hook your energy right into the earth. A grounding exercise can help here too.

Now bring your awareness back to your body and reconnect into your responsible adult self. How big are you? How much space are you taking up in the world? Are you shrinking away or can you expand? With every breath, imagine your energy field is expanding. If there's something in your life that's making you feel small (a person, or a project, or even just something in general) imagine that you can now grow bigger than it in your mind, as you breathe and expand. Breathe in certainty and strength; breathe out your fear, your smallness, your apologetic self. Let the fear and small feelings flow through your body and out through your feet. Come into balance. See yourself standing tall. Whatever it is, you can do it. Say out loud, "I can and I will." How does that feel? Let go of the images but hold on to the feeling. Know you can reconnect to this feeling anytime.

If you like saying "I can and I will," you can set it as a label on your phone alarm to go off in the morning. Or you can write it down on a Post-it and put it in the car. Get a mug with it as the slogan, or choose another slogan to hold the energy for you while you integrate and consolidate and allow yourself to become the responsible adult that you are.

Ceremony to Honor Your Inner Child Work

After the conscious and subconscious work, you need a period of time to process, consolidate, and integrate it. Once you feel you've moved on from the old patterns and your inner child is healing nicely, has become an ally, or has integrated with your adult self, it's time to mark the moment with a milestone. This can be a celebration or a ceremony. Here is a list of some things you can try. Because it's inner child work, it doesn't all have to be serious and formal.

Ideas for you to use to mark the growth and healing of your inner child:

- Have that birthday party you didn't have.
- Go see the movie your dad forgot to bring you to.
- Walk on the beach and throw stones or go fishing.
- What can you do with your own children that you wished you had done as a child?
- Buy yourself a teddy bear.
- Make your favorite dinner you had when you were small.
- Visit the places your grandad took you to that you loved so much.
- Invite your best friends over for a sleepover party (don't forget the popcorn).

Ceremony work helps you say, "Yes, I have done this work now," so you don't question it inside yourself. You know deep down that you have changed, that something has left you and something new has opened.

You have done great work. It doesn't ever stop, though; as long as you are alive, your inner child will be alive inside you too. So spend as long as you need to with the work of your inner child. They deserve the love and attention that you now know how to give to yourself. Just think—you were a child for at least twelve years, so if it takes two or three years to really do the work, isn't it worth it?

Enjoy the blossoming of all the relationships around you as the people you deeply care about become free to be the people they are instead of having to be the people that you need. And be secure in the knowledge that you will never be abandoned, as you have now learned how to give yourself the love you need.

Chapter 2

Your Inner Teenager

In this chapter I will look at how to heal the wounding that you may have received as a teenager, aged between twelve to nineteen years old.

I encourage you to bring your inner child with you into this chapter, as sometimes the stubborn teenager in us needs some fun, as well as love, to rouse them into opening up enough to be able to talk about what's going on for them.

Do you remember being a teenager? Your body goes through hormonal changes, school suddenly gets more serious, and friendships change. You find attractions and petty jealousies all around you. Trying to please everyone, your teenage self just longs for space to rest and play, but slowly the realization develops that childhood has truly gone but the independence of adulthood is still out of reach.

My inner teenager doesn't want me to write this chapter. She's sulking (even though I bought her an expensive candle), and I can see her in my mind's eye with her arms folded. She won't

43

meet my eye. "I'm not going to help you," she says, with her foot tapping, looking like she can't wait for the first opportunity to make a quick getaway. Welcome to the world of the inner teen, who can be your most valuable asset … or turn into your greatest enemy.

I pour the freshly boiled water into my cup, no expense spared: this rooibos tea is in a gossamer pyramid bag, full of the brew's leaves and bits of bark—no ground-up rubbish for my inner teen. "Come," I say, "sit and sip some tea with me. Tell me what's on your mind. What are you afraid of?"

She takes a step forward, hesitates, is about to step backward, and then changes her mind. She shrugs her shoulders and reaches out for the tea. "It's too hot," she says. "Wait a moment," I say to her. "You teenagers, so impatient, wanting everything now. It's okay to wait, to rest, to just be still." "But Dad says if I'm not doing something then I'm wasting my time." Ah, now she's opening up to me, just as your inner teenager will open to you. But just like me, you may have to lure them in, coax them into comfort, develop trust. Being a teenager is hard.

I sit with her for a while, not talking, just being there. She sips the tea. Breathe out. Relax.

Just like your inner child, your inner teenager will act out from time to time through your behavior. When you're in it, catching it is much more difficult than when you're coming from the space of a wounded child, because teenagers hide their wounding much better than children do. We all become our own worst enemies, so if you know yourself at all, you'll know the best way to hide yourself from yourself. Things like your true feelings about something or your frustration could be expertly hidden under a floorboard in a dark corner of your subconscious mind. You could be hiding an addiction from yourself, or even a true love. The part in the teenager that allows for magic often dries up when reality strikes. Hopes and dreams can be lost, depression can set in. Teenagers sit in an awkward limbo state between being child and adult, where perhaps they long to hug a teddy rather than dress up for a club, where a feeling of being overwhelmed at the amount of homework and study sets in and the need to please by excelling in extracurricular activities can become a tipping point for mental imbalance.

The aspect of you that is your inner teen is a part of you that is dynamic, amazing, beautiful (but probably doesn't know it), weird in the best sense of the word, wise, and fascinating, but without an audience to appreciate them, so they stopped talking long ago. The creative part of your inner teen is mostly undiscovered and became well hidden from you somewhere along the way. You the adult cannot recognize it in yourself anymore, and it's a shame. However, we are here to heal your inner wounds, and this is part of it—not recognizing how amazing you are, hiding in the bushes rather than stepping out, feeling that sense of shyness, or not feeling worthy/good enough. And of course, body image and self-esteem are a big part of the work as well. I'll tap into all of these issues in this chapter, so all you need to do is bring your inner teenager along with you. Believe me, that is going to be a difficult enough job.

Your Inner Teenager Wants to Be Loved

Just like the inner child, the inner teen needs love, only they don't want to admit it. They think they can handle everything by themselves, but when they fail, they berate themselves for their failings. They cannot make a mistake, yet in their own mind, mistakes seem to be all they can make.

In therapy work over the years there has been much work devoted to the inner child, but not so much to the inner teen. I first discovered my own inner teen when I found myself going into cycles of self-loathing and despair. By connecting to the me I was at fourteen, I was able to find that part of myself that always doubts, that is sneaky and hides, that dreams big dreams then burns it all up in flames. I reminded her of how resourceful, creative, and resilient she was as well as how protective of me she also was. She liked being acknowledged and admitted that yes, she was creative, but never had the space to blossom. When I got in touch with my inner seventeen-year-old, I found someone much more self-assured but still stubborn. She had very fixed ideas of the world, insisting things were this way, not *that* way, and not really wanting to hear logic or reason otherwise. I spent time listening to her and reminded her of how difficult her life was at that time, and showed her all the things she did achieve, rather than wallowing in shame about the things she never got to complete. She agreed to work with me to try hating herself a little bit less, and over a longer period of time, she was able to appreciate herself and let go of her anger.

We all have parts of ourselves we don't like, and it's usually this part of us, the teenager part. How our inner teen is formed really depends on what was going on in our lives at that time, and this chapter may stir up some memories and emotions that you may find difficult. But that emotional difficulty is the crux of this book—keeping these memories and emotions as unfinished business hidden somewhere deep inside our subconscious holds us back from life. So when you're making space to read, *really* make some space to read. Just as I found an expensive candle and poured an elegant cup of tea, ask yourself what you can do for your inner teen so they help you do the work rather than shut down or fight it.

Exercise

Journaling

List three things that you can do for yourself right now that would help you settle in more with the material presented here.

List three reasons you may *not* want to do these three things. Now work out how you can come to an agreement to work together with your inner teenager.

List three things that you would do for yourself to appreciate your inner teenager if time, space, and money were no issue.

Is there any way you can make any of these things happen? What else is in the way of this?

Healing our inner teen is a similar process to healing our inner child in that we get in touch with the teen and speak to them, find out what is going on with compassionate listening, discover what they didn't receive and why they're stuck in space and time. Then we try to give them what they need as best as we can. Over time, trust is built up, the separation between our adult personalities and the teenage personality dissolves, and we become the true embodiment of ourselves, i.e., the teenaged me at seventeen is no longer separated from me but instead lives inside me—age is no longer a variable.

The issues your inner teen brings to the table are not only personal but existential as well. Our teenage selves have more of an awareness of what the outside world is like, but remember that their ideas are filtered depending on the culture they were brought up in, their family values, the amount of exposure to outside media, and education. The inner teen is also beginning to step away from the idea that mother and father are "gods" and realizes that they are just people and can make mistakes. This realization can bring anger with it, as finding out something you based your foundation for life on is not true can overturn your idea of what the world is like—rebuilding is a big job.

A client told me in a session that her teenage daughter was viciously angry with her and said, "I wish you were more like Sarah's mother! She's normal! She does normal mother things. And she doesn't wear the same style clothes as Sarah, and she doesn't like the same music—it's like you're trying to *be me*! Stay away from me!" The poor woman was upset, and once she realized that it was a boundary issue, we knew where to put the healing. It eventually settled down, and now mother and daughter are able to be friends, to a degree. Teenagers need lots of time and patience, and we need to find that for our inner teen too.

In adolescence, you start building a stronger foundation regarding what is right and wrong, what is good or bad. To test this foundation requires a lot of judgment and criticism. It is on this foundation we solidify our ideas, unfortunately resulting in the creation of limited beliefs based on low self-worth that lingers well into adulthood. Our main personality affinities/tendencies show up in our teenage years as well. Do we see the glass as always empty, or always full? That can depend on what is going on at home.

Teenagers are able to compare what goes on at home to what goes on in other people's homes, something that younger children don't really do to the same degree. Some teenagers realize that certain behaviors of their parents that seemed normal to them over the years are actually not appropriate. It can be a time of big wake-up calls in households where there is trauma and abuse. Realizing that Mother is manic-depressive and Father is an alcoholic (where before it was just Mother being upset or Father having a few drinks) can change a person's world view. Though most of my clients would not have even realized this until they were in their twenties and repeating the behaviors with their own partners, some teenagers know something is wrong at home and feel powerless to do anything about it. If this is you, it's okay. It can all still be healed. In order to heal something though, you have to be able to name it.

In my client work, I find that the inner teen is the one we call on when I work with empaths who are exhausted from helping too much. Some teens get stuck with huge amounts of responsibility way too early, particularly in households where the parents are not functioning to their full potential. I also have found that the inner teen is the aspect of us that struggles most with life, friendships, and how to put their best foot forward or make a good impression. They usually end up putting on a mask for the outside world (or in fact many different masks), depending on who they are with. This is done as a form of protection, but it's also a way to hide what they feel is the truth—they believe they are not worthy so they must pretend to be.

It's the teen who wants to rebel against the machine, seeing where there is wrongdoing and injustice. Adults spend a lot of energy keeping that aspect quiet to hold down their day job, for example. Of course the teenager is used to not being listened to and can wither away completely over time, taking all of that magic and joy with them . . . or they can explode with rage causing illness, depression, and nervous breakdowns.

The inner teen is a complicated aspect of us. In order to get the most out of this chapter, you will need to take a step back and regard your teenage self as an observer, remembering how you behaved as well as how you felt at this age. You can take a risk and ask a family member what you were like when you were a teenager if you want. Why is that a risk? Well, I find that family members see you in a different way than you do, so asking them usually gives you something totally different than you expected, and it's not always pleasant. Do remember, though, that family projects themselves onto family, so there will be a filter in their answer depending on what was going on for them at that time too. Know that you don't need to run to a therapist and relive *all* the experiences you had as a teenager. Work from a foundation of compassion, love, and knowing that whatever manner your inner teen sees themselves now (even if it doesn't match the reality of when you were an actual teen) is the way to heal that aspect of you.

The Work of the Inner Teenager

Not all of the exercises here will fit for you, and that's okay. Everyone is different and has different experiences. Read through them all before you decide where to start, but do the first exercise so that you get familiar with who you were and what you may need to heal now. You'll know straight away which of the other ones you need to do and the order in which they should be done. Once you clear one piece of work with your inner teen, you may find that new levels and layers surface in you and an exercise that you thought was not relevant suddenly becomes the most important one for you to do next. Keep an open mind, and above all, go gently. Our inner teen is more delicate than they'd like us to believe.

Who Were You When You Were a Teenager?

It can really help if you can put your inner teen into context before you begin. Remembering where you lived, what was going on for you and how vulnerable you might have been can enlighten you in the work we will do here. Do it from two perspectives: what was going on outside of you and what was going on internally.

Where do you start? Our teenage phase spans almost ten years. Young teens are quite different from older teens, yet youth is still very much what is in common on both ends of the teenage spectrum. A eighteen-year-old doesn't necessarily know what is best for themselves, and sometimes a thirteen-year-old can have a very mature and responsible attitude. And of course there can be significant differences between your thirteen-year-old and eighteen-year-old depending on your life circumstances.

Exercise

Asking for Permission

Which teenaged aspect of you needs healing today? Close your eyes, relax, bring yourself into the room. Remember that you're the one in charge of you, not the teenager part, so you need to bring your responsible adult self here into the work to set the boundaries, decide how deep you need to go, make room to cry, and close it down when it's enough.

Knowing that the earth is beneath you holding you, pull your awareness away from all the other people in your family. Bring your awareness into your body: become aware of the weight of your arms, feel your feet pushing into the floor.

Now, say out loud or in your mind, "I give myself permission to work with my inner teenager. What do I need to do to get them to work with me?" Breathe and stay with this. Soften your heart to yourself. See which age they are when they show up for you. That's where you begin.

Say thank you to the part of you that showed up, and tell them, "I'm going to do some research to remind myself of all the things you were going through, but is there anything in particular you'd like me to remember?" See if they'll talk to you. If they will, listen with an open heart. You can write it down if you want, but it is very important to be impartial. Listen to them speak in their own words, voice their frustrations, get whatever they need to off their chest. There's no criticism here, just listening with love. Doing this could be difficult, which is why you need to be ready for it.

When your inner teen has finished speaking, thank them for their honesty and openness. Let them know how much you care about them and that you're really going to make the commitment to sort things out. And if you're able to, embrace them in your mind's eye. At the very least, offer a hand to shake. Allow a feeling of peacefulness to come in between you both. This could be the first time anyone has ever given this part of you the floor for speaking in your own words and without interruption for so long. It means a lot to this part of you too.

Cast Your Mind Back

This is more of a fact finding mission than a heart opening exercise. Make sure you won't be interrupted while you do this; you could be excavating difficult memories that come with difficult emotions, and you don't want to lash out at anyone who startles you while you're working.

Exercise

Remembering

With your notebook and pen in hand (and a nice cuppa beside you), cast your mind back to the age of the aspect of you that showed up for the first part of this exercise. That's the age you need to be for this part of the work. So if you were sixteen, focus on what you were like at sixteen and prepare yourself to go deep.

The memories may flow … or they may not. Because teenagers really don't notice everything or pay a lot of attention to things they're not interested in at the time, you can assume that you will never have all the information. That's okay; as I said earlier you probably don't need absolutely all the details, though some could be the missing pieces of a puzzle that can really help you heal. So as the responsible adult you are, become the impartial investigator and gather information as best as you are able in adult mode. In other words, don't *become* that aspect of you while you do this research. If you're stuck, try asking yourself these questions and write down the answers:

- What did you look like as a teenager?
- What type of clothes did you wear?
- How did you style your hair?
- Were you proud of how you looked or did you hide?
- What was it like for you at school?
- What type of relationships did you have with your classmates?
- What types of things did you like to do outside of school?
- Who were your friends? Who was your most important friend?
- Did you socialize a lot with friends or were you at home most of the time?
- Did you prefer to spend time alone?
- What was your home life like?
- How old were your brothers and sisters? What were they like? What kind of relationship did they have with you?
- How did you get along with your parents/grandparents?
- What was going on in your house? Were there problems at home?

- Did your parents go through a breakup while you were a teenager?
- How did this affect your adult view on relationships?
- Did you have all the information you needed to understand what was going on at the time?
- As the adult now, do you know more about what went on while you were a teenager?
- How does that make you feel about your teenage self?

Yes, this is a very difficult exercise, but painting the picture is part of understanding why your inner teen is acting out the way they do, through you when you are weak, tired, or exhausted. Your behavior and experiences explain the lack of communication, why they won't help you, or why you feel so angry sometimes for no apparent reason. And answering these questions really helps you come to terms with your joy and the magic in your life to pinpoint if or when it was extinguished, allowing you to rebuild your life and incorporate magic into it so it will never be lost again.

Working with Your Inner Teen

It's time to meet your inner teen and have a good heart-to-heart. By making a relationship with this aspect of yourself when you feel as though you're in a relatively good place, you get the connection activated so you can go to it when you are not. Responsible adults get moody too, sometimes turning inward and wanting to withdraw. It's also just as possible that adults feel like they want to rebel, turn outward, and scream at the world. How do you act when you're acting out of your inner teen?

Exercise

Meet Your Inner Teen

Just as we did in the inner child work, we need to make a space to meet our inner teen, though it might not necessarily be in nature.

Close your eyes and breathe, relax, and set your intention to meet your inner teen and find out what's going on for them. Spend a while going into your body, breathing out tension and anxiety before you begin, then when you're ready, go into a space in your mind's eye where you feel safe and can facilitate the work. Instead of you choosing where to meet, imagine that you're walking into a white room. Let the room furnish itself, and when it has revealed itself to you, make yourself comfortable and make space for your inner teen to visit you.

They're probably already there. Have a chat with them, listen to what they have to say—as difficult as it may be, make the effort to listen to them. Don't judge, jump in, or fix anything. Simply be compassionate and listen with an open heart. If there's anything you want to offer, wait until they've finished speaking.

Now ask what you can do for them. Reassure them that they're doing better than they realize and that you know how difficult it is for them. Embrace if you can, shake hands, or try to come to an agreement. And if you can't, the fact they met you at all is progress.

Let them go and dissolve the room away. Come back to yourself where you are.

What did you learn? If it's your first time meeting yourself at that age, you may need to do it a few times before trust is built up, and that's what this is all about. Even if all your inner teen does is scream and shout at you, let them get it out without interrupting them or needing to be right. That in itself is huge progress—remember, they've been holding it in for all these years and need to get it out, even if the pain they old isn't the truth of it. Promise yourself that you will never ever give up on yourself. How does it feel to say "I will never ever give up on myself" out loud? Your inner teen needs to feel safe before they will be able to listen to your now-adult take on it. So work on allowing all the aspects of you to feel safe with you first. Perhaps you need to do some work on that as the responsible adult as well.

Healing the Core Teenage Wounding

Take some time to recall instances when you the adult acted out of your inner teenager. It could be very subtle, and you could have missed it. Moods come and go, but sometimes one hangs around for longer than you would expect it to, pushing you to overreact or withdraw inward. For example, what about that time you got angry at the waitress because she brought you the wrong coffee and you yelled at her, or that time you almost hit your manager at work because he wasn't listening to you? Those are the types of events where you may be acting out of an inner teenage wound. It could also be more subtle—poor boundaries related to saying yes when you really wanted to say no … or saying no when you wanted to say yes. All of this counts.

The inner teen wounding stems from not listening or not being heard, not listening to yourself and your inner knowing, or feeling ignored and wanting to rebel. It's also not wanting to fit in or wanting to fit in—all are parts of forming your identity. Remember that we are here to heal the deeper wounding behind the behavior, so let's look at that here. Remember that for responsible adult you, making time to listen and hear is a natural way of being.

What comes up for you if you think of your deep teenage wounding? I'll be looking at bereavement in the next chapter and going into that in more detail. Let's look here at identification of the self, trying to fit in, noticing what other people are doing, and cutting off pieces of ourselves as teenagers so we can be accepted by the group. Does that fit for you? You've done a lot of work already on this now, so name the wound and write it down on a page. It will be different for everyone but that doesn't matter. It's the giving of permission and the setting of intention to heal that really helps.

The best thing you can do is still and ground yourself into the present moment as much as you can, as then you will become accustomed to how it feels and notice when you veer off course. There are plenty of books about how to do that (some are listed in the appendix), but we are mainly here to heal deep inner wounding. Now that you know where I'm coming from, ask yourself: What was going on for me as a teenager? Where are the wounds?

The Energy Work

If there was a core wounding that happened to you while you were a teenager, can you name it? Let's do some energy work on it—pure energy work this time. Invite your inner teen to receive healing too. Visualize them in your mind's eye. Notice their body language: Are they wanting to join in or do they still have unfinished business with you? If there is more to say and hear, do that first.

Make space for this exercise. Read it first before you begin it. You can do it with your eyes open; as you read each word, allow the energies to come into your energy field or you can record it on your phone and play it back to yourself (make sure you give yourself plenty of time in between sentences so you can allow the healing to happen). Remember you can check out my website for recordings and bonus material relating to this book: www.healyourinnerwounds.com

Exercise

Core Teenage Wounding Healing Visualization

Sit, breathe, and relax. Come into the moment, come into your body. Make sure you won't be disturbed. If you wish, you can play some relaxing music, and have nice smells near you and a blanket if you get cold.

Set your intention to heal. Say the following out loud: "I set my intention to heal my inner teenage wound." (If you can, name the wound—the more context, the better; you can also simply allow yourself to feel where it hurts and ask for the hurt to be healed.) "I release my need to hold onto my wound. I release my need to control." (Elaborate here if you can.) I surrender to the universe and invite the healing energies to come and heal my wounds for the highest good of all. I ask the aspect of myself that needs healing the most today to show up and also receive the healing."

If there's anything in the way of this, you need to know. So be open to any messages. If you need to stop here and clear the obstruction, then do so.

Breathe and relax. Close your eyes and let the visualization bring you where it will. Here's a rough framework you could use, but the energies will show you what you need to know.

Imagine you're surrounded by light. See your inner teen sitting beside you also surrounded by light. The more you relax, the more healing you will receive. Be with any emotion that comes up for you. This is difficult work, so give yourself as much time as you need and go as deeply as you are able. See yourself and your inner teen in a chamber of light. There are two beds in this chamber, one for each of you. You are both surrounded by beautiful light beings who are tending to the two of you. Simply notice the colors and lights, and let your body relax even more as they work. When it's over, simply let the image dissolve away and return to the present moment.

When the healing is complete, turn to your inner teen. See what they look like to you. Are they crying? Laughing? Smiling? Are they an ally and a friend to you now, or do they still have an issue with you? Listen to what they have to say. As difficult as it might be, open your heart to yourself as a teenager. Remember how tough it was, and know you did the best you could. You really did.

Is there any forgiveness work you need to do? Did you as a teenager do or say something that you've never forgiven yourself for? Did you behave in a way that you still don't understand? Are you able to forgive yourself now? If not, ask for healing to go to the part of you that's holding onto the unforgiveness. Do the exercise on values (later in this chapter), and then come back to this and try again.

Feel the light activating in your heart, the light of love. In silence now, see the heart light of your inner teen also light up. Feel the love flow from you to them, and back to you again. Embrace if you can, feel that you're reaching a new understanding and level of communication. Together you can do anything. Separated, you will tear yourself apart. Thank your inner teen for coming and receiving the healing too.

Spend some time sitting in the new energies of healing. If you want, take up your pencil and notebook to journal about the healing, what you felt, and how you are feeling now. Notice how it feels between you and your inner teen. Is there more love flowing? Be with that.

This might seem like a very simple exercise with very little power in it. However, only reading this and deciding against doing it because it is so simple is not how you make a commitment to heal yourself! Try it. Really go into it—make the space to try it. Especially go into the forgiveness aspect of the work. Know that you're being held in time and space and that the time for this healing work is now. By setting a deep intention and giving 100 percent permission to heal this, you are already healing it. Notice what changes in your life after you try this exercise—and yes, you can use anything as the premise for this pure energy work healing session. All you have to do is your work.

Release Your Masks

Your inner teen would have shapeshifted their personality depending on who they were with so that they could fit into the crowd. It's as if they had a mask for every situation in order to be accepted and blend in. We as adults can continue to wear these masks not only to blend in but also as comforting protection to hide behind. As we grow with these masks, they allow us to avoid showing our true selves to the world. We can lose who we are behind masks we use to the extent that we forget who we are underneath. We don't seem to realize that we don't actually have to show all the parts of ourselves to any one person. Not ever. Please be with this fact for a moment. Let it sink in.

Even as my best healed self I don't expose all of me to the world. There are parts of me that I believe are just for my family and not for public consumption, and there are parts of me that are just for me. As with clothing, underneath I am still me but how much of me I reveal depends on what clothing I choose to wear. It's important I point out here that what I wear is not a mask because I am not hiding; I don't worry about what people think of me anymore and don't need to put on a brave face or wear a mask to pretend to be something I'm not. I don't need to please everyone, and when you think about how many people exist in the world, you will realize too that no matter what you do, you'll never please everyone anyway. So why bother? Me, I'm very confident in myself and who I am. I want to help you get to this point too, and you can.

We start making these masks, or facades, when we are teenagers, if not before. The teen is an expert chameleon, able to change shape at any moment to fit into their surroundings. They create masks to place over their true selves so they become the person that pleases the people they are with. Over time, because the masks work and are used so often, they solidify so that eventually these facades take over, and the sense of self diminishes. I had a client once who had so many masks they became different personalities. She came to me because she couldn't remember which mask she was supposed to wear with which person and had lost herself somewhere along the way. Her situation became so serious that it lead to her having a breakdown. This is important work so don't underestimate it. Give yourself time and space to heal this, and know that it could take you six months to a year to feel safe going out without a mask. Be gentle and kind to yourself, and only do as much as you can.

There are several parts to the following exercise; you can take a few days to do one part each day, or you could do one part over several days going as deep as you can. Read the whole thing first so you know what is being asked of you. Prepare and get your own (and your inner teen's) permission, and gather all the materials you need. Keep in mind that it really is more powerful if you *do* it rather than simply think about it (yes, I'm talking to your inner teen here) but if you really don't want to make a mask, you can draw it on a page.

Part 1: Presentation
Start by creating actual masks that symbolize who you are when you're wearing them. Have fun with this, get some art materials together—big sheets of paper, drawing pencils, crayons, paint, stickers, glue, anything you have at hand, *or* go treat yourself in an art and hobby shop. You will need an afternoon for this, so

make a date with yourself in your diary and keep it. Invite your inner teen to come and give you artistic advice. Have fun with this! Keep it light but know that the healing is serious.

Exercise

Revealing Your Masks to Yourself

You can buy a blank mask in an art shop or you can draw the outline of a mask on a page that would be big enough to cover your face. Put in holes for eyes. Put it in front of your face and check for size.

Now, how many masks do you need? Now is the opportunity to heal, so really think about this. You can make the mask you wear for your friends, the one you wear at work, and another for when you are with your family. What other masks do you have? List them all out first, and make them all. Take as long as you need to do this.

Front of the mask: Hold the blank mask in your hand. Set your intention to draw the mask that you have chosen (e.g., the work mask). Place yourself in your mind's eye in the environment you have chosen, and feel the energy in your body change so you are holding yourself as you do in that environment. Breathe in and out, and be the you that you are when you are in that place with those people.

Now use your colors to create the mask the way you believe other people in the world see you. Use symbols, words, and choice of color to help you. Stay in the energy of the mask you have chosen. So if it's your work mask, color it the way you believe they see you at work.

Back of the mask: Stay in the energy of the environment you have chosen. When you flip the mask over, imagine that you're going deeper inward, behind the mask. Feel how your body really feels when you are in that environment. Don't hide your feelings from yourself; this is how you heal them. Color the mask in the way that you feel when you are wearing that mask—all of it, no holds barred. Use symbols, words, choice of color just as before.

Take a break in between each mask to clear the energy—do a dance, go for a walk, get a fresh cuppa—whatever you like. Then come back and do the next one. Though it's a lot of work, make sure your teenager stays with you while you work. When you've finished all your masks, take a proper break. Your teenage self might want to go lie down and listen to music for a while…and you might want to join them.

Part 2: Analysis

You may need to have a change of scenery before you start this part of the healing—go for a walk, do some shopping, or finish some household chores to give yourself a good transition space between parts 1 and 2. When you're ready, know that you are your own best analyst, so leave your inner teen upstairs with their headphones on, pour yourself a cuppa, and sit in stillness. Come from an analytical place of mind but also from a gentle healing space so that your emotions won't upset the cart. Reassure yourself that you're safe before you begin.

Exercise

Analyze Your Masks

Place all the masks you made face up somewhere where you can see them all at once so you can analyze them. What is the first thing that you notice?

As the impartial observer, study the different masks you made. See what the similarities are, see what the differences are. It is what it is; there is no need for judgment. Notice if they're all quite similar but in different ways. Are you drawing the same symbols on the masks but in different colors? What do you notice about the intention you have for each mask? Are all the intentions the same? Write this down so you don't lose it.

Now it's time to see what is behind these masks. You can choose one and flip it over and compare it to all the faces of the other masks. You can flip them all at the same time and see if they're all completely different from each other or if they're similar. You're the responsible adult, so you get to choose how to do this.

Here are some ideas:

- Compare the back of one mask to the fronts of all the other masks.

- Compare all of the backs of the masks to each other.

- Compare all the fronts of the masks to each other.

- Compare the front of one mask to the backs of all the other masks.

You get the idea. When you have analyzed the masks thoroughly, see if you can answer the following questions:

- What is the main theme going on in all the masks, front and back?

- What are the main discrepancies between the different masks, front and back?

- Which mask is the most different from the others? Why?

- Do you think you could amalgamate a few of the masks together and reduce the total number of masks?

Ask the universe: What would it take for me to feel safe to be myself with everyone I come into contact with in all environments, at all times?

Part 3: Healing

We heal by allowing ourselves to feel what we feel. And by bringing our awareness to our feelings, they change. You may need some time to heal this as it's quite a big thing, and if your masks are all completely different to each other, you may want to take some time to heal, and then repeat part 1 of the exercise again to see what has changed.

Exercise

Becoming Your True Self

When you feel safe to feel what you feel, choose one mask and hold it in front your face. Notice what happens to your energy. Imagine yourself in that environment with the mask on. Now turn the mask so that the inside is facing outside. What happens to your energy? Stay with it. Know that you don't have to do anything else right now and you already *are* this but are just neutralizing a fear of showing yourself. You don't have to show all the parts of yourself to anyone. Promise yourself that you will meet all of your own needs and that you do not have to hide parts of yourself from yourself. After all, you've just seen all of your inner feelings on the back of the masks—is there anything else you've been hiding from yourself?

Notice how you feel. Take the mask away from your face and hold your energy stable—is it difficult to do? Own the energy of what is going on in that mask; make it a part of you. Notice what doesn't fit—are you really trying to be something you are not? If so, why?

Put on a different mask. How different does this one feel? Take turns wearing all the masks front side out to notice if your energy shifts with each one. The more you repeat this exercise, the more you tune your energy in to what you think you need, and the less you will need the mask.

Which masks don't fit you anymore? Is discarding them a risk? Have you grown out of your job? Out of a relationship? These old masks can make you feel small—allow yourself to face the facts of it. Know you don't need to make any decisions. As long as you don't shrink in your life, you can do so much more and it won't hurt as much.

You could imagine all the masks amalgamate into one mask. You can feel it energetically or draw a new all-encompassing mask if you like. You could also try burning the masks though again—it's up to you. What you can do depends on where you are on your journey and how ready you believe you are to do this part of the work. You could check in with your inner teen to see how they're doing and if they have any advice for you.

In my experience, the fear to be yourself completely is the fear that you will be angry, you'll lash out at someone, and say or do something you will regret. It is the fear that you'll get hurt or that someone will judge you and not like you. It's also the fear that you own your power and will then have to do something with it you're not already doing. We will cover this in later chapters.

Life will always throw things at you—it's your challenge, and to learn and grow is why we are here. What helps? Having a daily spiritual practice. When you are connected to yourself most of the time, you naturally let go of anger; you come into the moment and feel safe, grounded, and present at all times. It's something to work on, not something that magically fixes itself just because you want to fix it. So if this resonates with you (and your inner teen is groaning because there's more work to do), it's probably exactly what you need to do.

Part 4: Embodiment

There's no point healing something and then slipping back into the old mental patterns. When you do this, you recreate the energy pattern that you just let go of; it feels like you've moved backward but in truth you've created something new—it just looks and feels the same as the old pattern. That's why embodiment is such an important part of the work. Here are some things to look out for and to keep in mind when you're in your day-to-day life and you notice you are putting those old masks on again.

Know the difference between needing protection and needing a mask

Perhaps what you actually need in a certain environment is not a mask at all but some form of protection. Try taking your mask off and being completely who you are. Then visualize energetic protection around you. The protection could look like a shield the knights of old had, a bubble of protection, or colors or lights. Make sure you are grounded and your energy field is big and strong. Remember too that a daily practice can really help with this. Notice the difference between not wearing a mask and setting up energetic protection, wearing a mask with protection, and just wearing a mask. Being able to tell the difference so you have awareness of what you're doing subconsciously and can heal if needs be will only help you.

Practice removing your mask

Notice how your energy feels when you're in an environment where you usually wear a mask. Quietly notice if you are wearing an energetic mask: ask yourself if you are and which one if so. Visualize it on your face, covering yourself up. How does that feel? Now take the risk and allow the mask to dissolve. Feel yourself expanding energetically as you release your need to hold yourself in a certain way and in a certain shape to please someone else. Keep doing what you do but note—has anything changed around you? Are people talking to you in a different way? Do you feel happier in yourself? If you feel anxious, perhaps you need to put the mask back on but with an awareness of it that means you're not hiding it from yourself anymore. That's a big difference and well done. Give yourself the time to grow out of it rather than force yourself to do something you're not ready to do. You could imagine the mask getting thinner; remember that this mask isn't a form of protection—it's your personality.

Swap the masks around

Another way you could embody this change is to swap your masks around so you're using different ones in different places with different people. Really feel the differences between each of your masks so you can get closer to amalgamating them into one mask. For example, you could try on your family mask while you are at work and see how it feels. Notice your energy configuration and how you're holding yourself in your body. What is in you that feels odd when you do this? Can you name it? Do you want to take the mask off, or would you prefer to put the work mask back on?

Check in with yourself regularly

If you're going into an environment where you know you put on a mask, ask yourself before you go there, "What do I need to do to protect myself so that I feel safe in that place?" Ask your inner teen; surely they're the one who knows the answer to this, and they'll be oh so delighted that you asked. Then do it—follow through. That's the beginnings of true embodiment.

Becoming Who You Are Means Not Being Jealous of Other People

Sometimes we use the masks to hide feelings of inadequacy that stem from comparing ourselves to other people ... or our ideas of other people. Know that the grass grows green where you water it. If you're not watering yours, and someone over there waters theirs, then of course their grass looks better than yours does.

The difference between being a teenager and being an adult is that the adult is totally responsible for all of their actions, while the teenager still needs the occasional kick in the backside to get moving. So the teenager sits with parched grass and admires the grass across the street, wishing *their* grass was as rich and as beautiful, but doesn't put the work in. Are you still doing this as an adult?

Looking at what other people have and admiring it to the point of jealousy is not a healthy thing to spend energy on. I love looking at pretty gardens and beautiful flowers, but I know that if I don't plant flowers in my own garden, I won't have any. I decided I did want flowers in mine, so I started planting them. But my inner teenager wanted to moan about it for a while. I let her and then said, "Okay, let's stop that nonsense and go to a garden center." I did find myself dragging my heels, but once I got there and saw what they had and what I could get, I was very happy.

The concept of bringing things in your life that you admire in other peoples' can apply to many parts of your life. I see jealousy as a signal that needs are not being met; jealousy left to fester can become anger, resentment, bitterness, and can eat away at your soul. So stop doing it. Pull your power back into yourself and sit with your inner teen; ask what is really going on at the core of it. For example, if the teenager wants the flowers but doesn't want to do gardening, explain that the flowers won't bloom. Maybe they don't actually want the flowers at all, and that's okay too. But until you sit down with yourself and have that conversation and find out what it is you're jealous of, you'll never heal it. Remember that your inner teen has insights that you may not have if you work without them.

Another aspect of jealousy can come from the apathy teenagers have around not wanting to do work. Everyone is or was a beginner at one time; even the people who are the experts of today had to start somewhere. So taking baby steps is a lot easier than racing to the finish line incomplete or resenting people you perceive as ahead of you.

Here's a visualization exercise that you can do to reclaim your power from the things you think you want and the people who make you jealous. Ultimately, nobody makes you feel anything—it's *you* allowing yourself to feel that way.

Exercise

Reclaim Your Power from People and Things

Bring your inner teenager with you for this one, see how they feel. Perhaps they need some convincing first.

Visualize the thing or the person that you are jealous of.

Notice how you feel when you imagine the object of jealousy in your presence. Is it something you want but don't want to work for? Is it something you feel you deserve but is not being recognized by the world?

See your essence as a beautiful light that has become trapped inside that person or thing due to your wanting.

See yourself wanting your essence back more than you want the thing or are upset with the person.

Neutralize how you feel about the thing—decide that you will work for it, talk to the person in your mind, and congratulate them for their achievements. Acknowledge what the person has done and what life has given them.

Now pull yourself inward to yourself. You have forgotten how amazing you are, how talented you are when you are allowed to be who you are.

You can work hard, and when your mind and heart are in alignment, you can have anything you want. Remind yourself of this.

See the light of your essence lifting out of the thing, of the person. Feel it coming back to you through space and time, accumulating in your energy field around your physical body, ready to come back to you.

Feel the weight of your essence as it gathers, and visualize it getting brighter. Ask for it to be healed and cleansed.

How is your inner teenager doing at this point? Have they dissolved into you? It's all okay and as it should be.

Feel your essence merging into your energy field. You are back. Your power has come back. With this power you can create anything you want. Without it, you long for it but in the guise of the thing it has attached itself to.

Remember this exercise if it was a powerful experience for you, and do it regularly.

Becoming Who You Are Means Consciously Being Aware of Your Values

Your values are the principles, beliefs, and attitudes that are important to you in the way you live and work. Your values are formed in your childhood and solidify during teenage years, but they can shift and move as you grow and change. Values come from your parents, culture, background, social status, education, place of employment, and experiences. They also are influenced by media, pop culture, famous figures, and music. We rarely take time to rethink our values so they could be stuck in time or out of date with where our hearts are now. These stuck or hidden values can become what are called *limiting beliefs*, which are difficult to shift and hold us back from reaching our full potential.

When the things you are doing don't align with your personal values, it affects how you feel about yourself. Teenagers shift their values to suit the group of people they're involved with; for example, I've had clients who got in with a bad crowd while being a teenager; they stole, did drugs, and convinced themselves that it was okay because the other people in the group were doing it too.

I used to work in a job where they told me it was more important to make something up than to tell the client that I didn't know the answer. That went against my values of integrity, so I couldn't tell lies to please my manager. I had a think about this and decided that instead of making up something, I would say, "I don't know the answer but it's a great question. Give me some time, and I will find the answer and get back to you as soon as I can." That was more in keeping with my values; I could live with it and my clients respected me all the more for it. Another example of how values can influence you is the Irish Catholic culture of not admitting your worth, not believing that anything that you made could be good. It's a value of pride, not allowing yourself to ever be proud of yourself. It's time to turn this around so that we can step into our power, be who we are and acknowledge what we have achieved.

Why look at values when doing work of the inner teen? Well, if you held one set of values as a teenager and another one now as an adult, it might be more difficult for you to understand why you did what you did when you were a teenager. That perspective can lead you into forgiveness work—where you truly believe that you did the best you could with what you knew at the time. There's another reason why it's important to look at values here: you may have created values based on your culture/family/education that are no longer suitable for your current state of being. Perhaps some of the limiting beliefs in your life that hold you back come from values you unknowingly created based on your experiences. such as "nobody could ever love me," "I'll never be able to finish anything," or "I'm not good enough."

Now you have an opportunity to refresh your own values as a positive step to becoming more authentically you. Look at your present life, how you live, what is important to you, and your values now. Perhaps you will gain a deeper understanding of yourself and be able to do some forgiveness work as a result.

Once you start thinking about your values, notice which ones you hold that you consciously decided upon and which you inherited. The exercise below helps you rank the values in order of importance as your inner teen, and as the responsible adult you are right now. You may decide to do further work with your values, and there is plenty out there that you can do; see the resources section in the appendix for guidance.

Exercise

Reevaluate Your Values

On a scale of 1 to 10, where 1 is not important at all and 10 is extremely important, rank the following. Compare and contrast your results. Do you get insight as to where you were then? Do you have more tolerance for yourself as a teenager now?

Value	Inner Teen Rank	Responsible Adult Rank
Fitting in with the group		
Being a leader		
Being a follower		
Being liked by others		
Helping others		
Being healthy and fit		
Being independent		
Wearing nice clothes		

Value	Inner Teen Rank	Responsible Adult Rank
Being a good parent		
Protecting the rights of children		
Standing up for injustice		
Having lots of money		
Being there for friends		
Being there for family		
Being proud of achievements		
Having a big house		
Getting married and having babies		
Traveling the world		
Reading lots of books		
Working to change society		
Wanting to change the world		

Value	Inner Teen Rank	Responsible Adult Rank
Keeping up to date with current affairs		
Leaving a legacy behind		
Being happy		
Working for someone else		
Working for myself		
Developing inner peace		
Looking after myself		
Always learning something new		

How do you feel looking at your value list? Did you gain a deeper understanding of how you have grown over time? Can you go back to the energy work part of this chapter and offer deeper forgiveness to yourself as a teenager? Though I've been speaking about it as though it were, your inner teen is not a separate entity. Your inner teen is you, just as all the parts of you that you show when you wear different masks is also you. It is easier to separate them to name the wounded parts so they can be healed.

Is there anything more that you need to do to heal this aspect of you? Sit with it. Honor your inner wisdom. Go to a therapist if you need to. The only one who can do your work is you.

Ceremony to Honor Your Inner Teen

What did you love to do as a teenager? What did you never get to do that you really longed to try? Is there something you can promise yourself and your inner teenager that you can do for them?

The ceremony can be anything from an elaborate ritual to something as simple as lighting a candle in silence. Remember that this is about your coming out strong, as the real you—who you actually are, no holds barred. So what would you like to do to celebrate being you?

Invite your friends or do this ceremony alone. Think for a moment and write down what you want to do, but make sure you do it. I won't give you any ideas here, just some guidelines and a gentle nudge to do it. Like the embodiment part of the work, we also have to honor how far we have come.

There was a lot to do in this chapter, so take time to honor your work. Perhaps what you'd like to do most is sit in the sunshine with a good book and just be at peace. Or maybe you wish to light a candle and dedicate the space to the work you've done.

Affirmations

Affirmations are statements that have deep meaning. They are powerful medicine with vibrations that influence your energy field. If you say a statement and don't believe it, the medicine it brings to you is not as powerful. I use affirmations as benchmarks. By saying one and being completely open to yourself—no masks, no hiding—you can get a reading on how deeply you believe it. It's not good enough to only do this with your mind, however—you need to do it with your whole body. Say an affirmation and feel it in your mind. Does your mind agree? Feel it in your heart. Does your heart agree? Feel it in your stomach. What does your instinct say to you? Then and only then do you know where you are with it.

Try saying the following affirmations to honor yourself and see where you are with the work you have already done. If there is more you need to do, you'll know because you won't be feeling these at 100 percent.

- I feel safe to be me.
- I will never abandon myself.
- I am able to look after myself.
- I have compassion in my heart for my inner teenager.
- I did the best I could with what I knew at the time.
- I forgive myself completely for the mistakes that I made.
- Not everyone has to like me and I am okay with that.
- I do not need to please everyone.
- I am allowed to say no to things.
- I can give myself everything I need.

Just like the work with the inner child, remember that you were a teenager for almost ten years, so you are not going to reverse wounding quickly. Repetition creates reassurance, so you will need to put the time and effort in. You're worth it, and so is your inner teen. If you don't believe that, then read this chapter again.

Chapter 3

Your Young Adult

In this chapter I will look at how to heal the wounding that you may have received as a young adult, aged roughly between twenty and twenty-six years old.

Just as you were encouraged to bring your inner child into the teenage years, I encourage you to bring both your inner child *and* your inner teen into this chapter. Recall that we are not straightforward and logical beings. The different parts of us bleed into each other, and all they want is to be seen, heard, validated, and loved.

There's a huge amount of freedom in reaching your twenties, but it can also feel very daunting. Depending on your life situation, experiences, values, and limiting beliefs, turning twenty can feel like…well, a bit of a letdown. No fireworks explode; nothing really actually feels any different than it did when you were nineteen.

For the first three to six years of your twenties, you're coming to terms with the freedom you have but also with the consequences of that freedom. You're not sure yet what it really means to be an adult, so going out and trying "adult" things is most definitely on the agenda. Overdoing it is commonplace, and many burn the candle at both ends to pack in as many activities as possible while eating badly, drinking too much coffee (or alcohol!), spending money they don't have, and putting off important things until the very last minute. On top of it all, you've slowly lost touch with most of your childhood friends and have fallen head over heels in love with the first person you met who told you that you're beautiful.

Ouch.

Let's get serious. We open our hearts to the world when we are in our twenties, hoping that someone/something will look after us, trusting that we are safe out there … and most likely we get our hearts broken. The daydreams we had in primary school are replaced with the reality that we have a hefty university loan to pay back, we may never get to become an astronaut, and the only job we can really take right now may be the one packing bags in the supermarket.

This chapter is about stepping back into the shoes you wore when you were in your twenties. (Do you remember your shoes? Mine hurt!) This is where the beauty and complexity of our personalities really starts to expand and deepen. Just like before, the work here is a process of you preparing and becoming willing to do the work, then taking some time to get back in touch with who you were then, painting the picture as to where you were in your life, what you were experiencing, what was painful for you, and how that pain transfers to you, right now, as the responsible adult you are. That said, we don't need to go look for pain and pick open old wounds. The process I have in mind here is a little different from how we have been working up to now.

I'm writing this chapter for you, the grown adult. I don't know what your wounding may have been during your twenties but you certainly do. For this reason, I'm offering a selection of different things that could have happened to you then, such as your first bereavement, a relationship breakup, a betrayal, and a violation of your boundaries.

The work we have covered so far includes the following:

- Stepping away from always being the caregiver
- Healing the wound of abandonment
- Learning how to receive love
- Being able to have fun without guilt
- Feeling seen and heard in the world
- Reclaiming the truth of who you are and releasing the masks
- Letting go of comparison and jealousy
- Refreshing your values to learn what is truly important to you

As I said before, we are not straightforward and we need repetition to heal. So if you find anything in your life that still comes up for you around these particular patterns, know that it's probably not the twenty-year-old who needs healing. If you find yourself acting out of wounding in a childish way (it's very hard to catch, but if you really are observant and nonjudgmental of yourself, it is possible), then it's your inner child who needs to be healed, not the twenty-something. However, it can be the twenty-year-old in you who took a another, deeper hit around a similar wounding—for example, if you experienced your first relationship breakup at twenty-one, your heart breaks, but somewhere in you there is a wounded, abandoned child who is also heartbroken and un-healed. You can heal both of these parts of you together if you make space to include them in your healing work.

Starting with Forgiveness

Knowing what you now know, can you forgive yourself com-pletely for any "bad" behavior that you think you carried out while you were in your twenties? Are there incidents and events that took place during those years that are still draining your power every time you think about them? If so, you need to do a forgiveness exercise for you back then, just like we did for the teenager.

Do the exercises in chapter 2 but bring your twenty-year-old with you instead. Go back in time to who you were, heal the core wounding, have another look at your values as they were then and compare them to yours now to really get an understanding of where you were with yourself back then. And do forgiveness work using this exercise here.

Exercise

Forgive Yourself for Everything

You might want to focus on a single event at a time, or you might be able to use this as a general forgiveness exercise. Repetition is good, slow is good, deep is good. Go easy on yourself—you truly did the best you could at the time with what you knew and understood.

Take the time you need to sit and relax your body and mind. Slow it all down. Set a timer if you need so you can really let go of anything on your mind. Whatever is occupying your attention can wait for when you're ready for it.

Set your intention to forgive yourself completely. Say the following out loud: "I set my intention to forgive myself for everything (or name one thing and take it one step at a time). I release my need to hold on to my emotional pain. I let myself off the hook. I understand that I did the best that I could with what I knew and understood at the time. I surrender to the universe and invite the healing energies to come and heal my wounds for the highest good of all. I ask the aspect of myself that needs healing the most today to show up and also receive the healing."

Breathe and relax. Close your eyes and visualize a safe space in nature where you can invite the aspect of yourself you wish to forgive to come and connect with you.

Wait and see who shows up. Remember to open it up so that if your inner child or inner teen is the one who appears, you're open hearted to them. Talk to them—say you've forgiven them, acknowledge that it wasn't their fault and they didn't know any better. Tell them you remember being there in that moment and there really wasn't anything else you felt you could do at the time. Tell them that you're doing great now, that you're ready to move on, and that you want their forgiveness too. Tell them you're sorry you held on to this emotional pain for so long and that with their help, both of you can let it go.

Feel the light activating in your heart, the light of love. In silence now, see the heart light of the aspect of you that showed up also light up. Feel the love flow from you to them, and back to you again. Embrace them if you can, and feel that you're reaching a new understanding and level of communication. Together you can do anything; separated, you will tear yourself apart. So thank this aspect of you for coming and receiving the healing too.

Spend some time sitting in the new energies of healing. Let the images dissolve away and be at peace for a while. If you want to take up your pencil and notebook, you could journal about the healing, what you felt, and how you are feeling now. Notice how it feels between you and the aspect of you. Is there more love flowing? Be with that.

When you look at the timeline of the wounding in your life you begin to realize that you need to track it back to the first level of wounding to truly heal it. The miracle is that the healing ripples from that point in time, the original wounding, to you now, in this present moment. It happens in layers, so keep in mind that perhaps you only healed one layer and need to go back to do more. Perhaps you need to track the wounding to the next level to release the pattern and live free of it from here on.

If you feel that your particular wound has not been covered in this chapter, that's okay. We will be looking at lots of other types of wounding in the coming chapters, including Divine Feminine (mother-daughter wounding) and Divine Masculine (father-son wounding). Perhaps your inner wound is so elusive that you need to go back to your child wounding or your teenage wounding and uncover deeper, hidden layers before you can actually name the primary wound. Either way, know that anything can be healed when you open your heart to yourself and every aspect of you is asking for healing to enter your life.

Bereavement and Loss

Perhaps you experienced bereavement as a child or teenager, something that happens to many of us. If that's the case, bring your inner child or inner teenager here instead of your inner twenty-year-old. As per all the work we have done so far, you—the orchestrator of the healing and responsible adult—know how deeply you can go and when it's time to stop and rest.

It's more difficult to do the work of bereavement when you have a closed heart, so let's start with healing that.

Healing a Broken Heart

Where do we start with a broken heart? Well, how do you feel? Be here, right now, in this moment, and allow yourself to feel the ground beneath you. Feel the sky above you. Know that you are safe. It is safe to feel how you are feeling.

Whatever the cause of your broken heart and the story of it, it's something that happened and is done now. You are here now, and it's time to heal this. So whether your broken heart came from a relationship breakup, the death of a loved one, the loss of a dream, the realization that you would have to work for a living, or if your heart has just closed softly and gently over time due to lack of joy, this healing is something you can repeat many times in a gentle way. I offer you now some gentle, loving healing for your heart regardless of what happened to you. For now, don't go into the story of your pain if you can help it. Stay with the heart, holding its hand, so to speak, and allow it to recover more fully.

As usual, read this exercise first before you do it. Make space. You can do it with your eyes open as you read each word; allow the energies to come into your biological energy field. Or you could record it on your phone and play it back to yourself (making sure you give yourself plenty of time in between sentences so you can allow the healing to happen). Remember also to check my website for recordings and related bonus material.

Heart healing is quite powerful if you give it time, space, and lots of compassion. Here are three techniques for pure energy healing that you can use to heal your heart. Try one or try them all but no matter what you do, give yourself time in between to let your energies settle and the healing to take hold.

Exercise

Journey to Heal Your Broken Heart

Make space and give permission for healing to take place.

Allow for pure energetic healing to come in. Say out loud, "I give permission for my heart to heal. Please can I be connected to a source of healing energy that can heal my broken heart?"

Step away from the story in your mind. You're doing pure energy work, so you don't want to remember *why* your heart aches. Just offer the pain up to the universe, open, and receive the healing light.

Breathe and relax; come into your body. Take as long as you need, and let the emotions come up (they most definitely will).

Visualize a space in nature where you can go to connect to your soul. See yourself walking there, imagine the textures and colors. Hear the sounds beneath your feet. Feel the weather and the wind. Smell the flowers. You want as much detail as possible.

Relax more. Go deeper. Find a lake and jump in! Let the water wash you clean of all the stress and fear you're carrying. Walk along the riverbank, feel the heat of the sun on your body as you dry. Lie down on the grass and open your energy field. Allow your emotional pain to release through your body into the ground, and feel it being taken from you into Mother Earth.

Feel your heart lighting up softly at first and then more strongly. As you breathe out, give the pain to Mother Earth. As you breathe in, feel the healing energies coming in at a deeper level.

Stay here for as long as you are able.

The slower you move, the deeper the healing, so give yourself plenty of time to return to the present moment after these healing sessions. This next exercise is another beautiful visualization that you can use for heart healing. Healing your heart takes time and repetition, so why not mix it up a little bit?

Exercise

Journey to Your Soul Garden

Make space and give permission for healing to take place.

Allow for pure energetic healing to come in, say out loud: "I give permission for my heart to heal. Please can I be connected to a source of healing energy that can heal my broken heart?"

Step away from the story in your mind. You're doing pure energy work, so you don't want to remember *why* your heart aches. Just offer the pain up to the universe and open and receive the healing light.

Breathe and relax; come into your body. Take as long as you need to prepare to do this work.

When you're ready, visualize yourself at the gatepost of a garden, the garden of your soul. Get permission to enter, open the gate, and step inside.

Notice how the garden looks: Is it cluttered and busy or organized and open? At the back of the garden is a flower, the flower of your heart. It wants to talk to you, so take your time but make your way through the garden to reach it. You can make adjustments to the garden if you wish. You can throw away rubbish, clear the weeds, and water some of the other flowers first, if you want to. Or you can do this before you leave and go visit your heart flower first. It's totally up to you.

Find your heart flower and notice what type of flower it is. Sit cross-legged in front of it and breathe with it until it feels like the flower is breathing with you too.

As you pay attention to your heart flower, it blooms. Its colors become richer, its petals fuller, and it smiles with you. It loves to see you. If it's in a bad way such as in a small, tight bud, that's okay. Just be with it as it is. Breathe with it, talk to it, tell it it's doing a great job.

The more you feed your heart flower with your attention, the more it will grow. Allow your heart in the visualization to light up and feed the flower with the light of your own compassion. You can also imagine you are watering it, weeding around the base of it, clearing debris away so that it can see the sunshine again. Remind your heart flower that it is important, that you care deeply for it, and that you want to help it. Ask it what it needs from you, if anything.

Stay there for as long as you need to. Feel your heart in your physical body shift as the flower shifts.

Smile and give thanks when you're ready to leave. Get up and notice the garden as you walk back the way you came. See if anything looks different or if you want to do some more gardening on the way to the gate.

When you step to the gatepost, again give thanks to the garden. You could imagine the sun is shining and the garden has become more beautiful, just because you have visited it. You can come back to the garden whenever you wish. Open your eyes and bring yourself back into the room.

You can do the main part of this exercise anywhere, anytime, for as long as you want. If you're feeling emotional, however, do give yourself a safe space to be in so you can allow yourself the privacy and boundary of safety. When you ask the questions, make sure you're somewhere where you won't be disturbed so you can tune in to yourself.

Exercise

Healing Your Heart in Real Time

Feel your feet on the ground. Bring your awareness to your hips, right and left equally. Feel your legs, strong like tree trunks, and the roots growing from your feet into the ground.

Bring your awareness into your stomach. Relax your stomach and let go of any emotional pain—breathe it out. Let go of tension, relax the muscles; again, breathe it all out.

Bring your awareness to your heart and say thank you to your heart. Let it know that you see it, that you're here for it. Tell it it's doing a great job and that you understand why it's feeling the way it is feeling, but you're here now and it is safe to heal.

Bring your awareness to the top of your head. Say in your mind or out loud: "Please connect me to the highest vibration of energy healing that I can hold today." Imagine a beautiful healing light connecting to the top of your head. The color of the light can vary depending on what you are needing at that time.

As you breathe, imagine you are drawing the light down from the top of your head, into your skull, into your neck, into your shoulders. Feel the light coming in and rolling down your arms to your wrists, then out of your hands. Imagine your hands are lighting up, and place one hand on your heart, the other on your stomach. As you breathe, the light comes further into your body so your heart receives healing from your breath and from your hands.

With every breath, know that your heart is receiving. Ask yourself if there is anything you need to know or do, or if there is any unfinished business that you need to take care of so that your heart can heal. Listen with your intuition, not your mind.

The Embodiment of Heart Healing: Trusting Love

When you have a broken heart, the part of you that loves freely closes up. When your heart has healed, it wants to love freely once more, but our minds are guarded against receiving similar hurt. And just as the healing I offer you is gentle, you need to be gentle with yourself and allow your heart to mend, taking the time that it needs to take rather than the time you *want* it to take.

We are made to share love with one another and to learn from each other, so refusing to invite someone into your life because you once had a broken heart can hold you back from the richness available to you. Know that your heart can love if it wants to love, but in order to be healthy love, what flows must be without manipulation, without expectation, without need.

We will look at this in much more detail in the chapters on the Divine Feminine and the Divine Masculine. If you cannot love without strings attached, you will need to do more work but you certainly can learn how to love that way if you really want to. For now, reassure yourself that love is not the thing that can hurt you; true love is not something you need to fear. People, on the other hand, are a different issue altogether. We are all sparks of consciousness just trying to make sense of the world as best we can with what we have.

You are beginning to see that a person is a multidimensional being. You've been doing a lot of work on the different aspects of yourself, and all people have different aspects of themselves that probably also need healing. It is likely that the other people in your life have not done their healing work. I hope this is not the case, but you doing your work can actually inspire others to do theirs, ideally as a natural progression without force or judgment. The light of your soul brightens as you heal; the quality of the light that you are improves and reminds people that you care and believe they can be that bright themselves. If they are willing to heal, they naturally drift toward doing things that will improve their light and their lives. Others being willing and making the choice to heal on their own is much more preferable (and subtle) than you thrusting a copy of this book into their hands and telling them that they have to do all the exercises in it!

Here's something that may help you work with other people out of the compassion and kindness bursting out of your healing heart, particularly if something someone has said or done has upset or disturbed you. See the whole person in their entirety—their personality that struggles through life, their eccentricities and behavioral patterns, their fixed ideas of how the world should be. Now take a step back and notice the soul that binds all of their different aspects together. They're wearing masks too, just like you may have been doing. So don't wrap your idea of who they are into just their personality or their behavior in the moment. When you step back, you create a space for you to begin to be able to love openly and wholeheartedly, allowing the soul of that person to be the main element and the other factors to be aspects of their character and personality. The very fact that this person exists and is in your life is something worth celebrating. As difficult as they may be to be around at times, you can always step away from the drama, the story, and their wounding to be with the bigger part of them. If you have trouble doing this, the exercise in this chapter called "Reclaiming the Parts of You that Left When the Relationship Ended" will really help you with this. You need to do your work, but know that your work heals others too.

The Safe Release of Grief

When someone you love dies or if a relationship ends, the grief comes no matter how prepared for it you think you are. Grief comes in all sorts of different ways depending on your personality, your wounding, your ability to process, and the relationship and soul contracts you have had with that person.

I had a client who was grieving for her father three years after he had died. She came to me because she was in such a state of intense grief and such a long time had passed that she thought there was something wrong with her. Her family had stopped empathizing with her and were telling her to "shape up and snap out of it," but she was so stuck in the grief she simply couldn't move on.

When we went back to the time her father died, she told me that his death was a shock to everyone and was totally unexpected. I dug a little deeper and discovered that my client stepped into her childhood pattern of caregiver, making sure her mother and her sisters were okay, making the funeral arrangements, and doing much of the background work that is needed when some-one passes away. It further transpired that six weeks after the funeral, she was back at work but still looking after her mother and had not made the space to grieve.

This is a normal occurrence, albeit not an ideal one. If the client's story resonates with you, understand that we have a huge capacity to bury or switch off feelings we carry deep inside of us and continue with what we call "real life." Over time, these buried feelings do not go away but instead become pressures within that grow over time, acting as a magnet that attracts similar heavy emotions, a little bit like a grain of sand in the oyster. You grow a pearl of grief that attracts more and more grief while getting on with your life, feeling heavier and heavier. The colors drain from the day, the joy is lost, and life becomes about just getting through it. Depending on the levels of stress and your resilience, it's only a matter of time before something bad happens and knocks you down for ten. You may fall ill, have a breakdown, or fall into depression; I know people who have become so badly affected by the buildup of unprocessed emotions that they end up on disability and cannot work or function in society anymore. It is not a way to live. If you can't picture yourself here, I'm sure you know several people who fit this description.

There was much more going on with my client. Recall that I mentioned soul contracts; these are the agreements between two or more souls made outside the levels of personality and ego, to learn lessons and be in a relationship with each other. You've probably heard of a soul mate—someone you have an instant connection with, where it seems like you've known them forever. Well, there are different levels of soul mate that could even include the bully in the schoolyard, whose soul agreed with yours that you'd not be friends in this lifetime but would be antagonists instead, to set you up for the bigger lessons you'd be learning as adults. Yes, it's true—your worst enemy, if you have one, is also a soul mate, just like your best friend, your children, or your lover.

We are learning about love. At the level of soul there is no animosity, only love. At the level of personality (all of those layers you built up over time and inherited) are fixed ideas, limiting beliefs, and a framework that may or may not clash with other people's fixed ideas, limiting beliefs, and framework. Like the mask exercise, you know how to present yourself to different people but are learning how to be who you truly are without the fixed limitations and the framework. You will always have an ego, however, and it is the part in need of the most love so it can shift and change as you grow and accommodate the love that is here.

Levels of soul mate get closer as we move into the inner circle of soul family—these are the people and souls who incarnate with you over many lifetimes. In this closeness, karma builds over the years when you didn't learn the lessons with a soul you said you would, necessitating your return and reattempt. If you want more detail on this I recommend Caroline Myss's classic work *Sacred Contracts*. My client and her father were top level soul mates who had been together through so many lifetimes and in different forms of relationship with each other. In this lifetime he was her father, in another lifetime she was his grandmother, in another lifetime he was her son, and so on. Though we never will know how many lifetimes we have lived with a soul mate, for my client, the loss of this man was greater than the loss of her father in a single lifetime; it could have been equivalent to the loss of five fathers over five lifetimes, and three sons over three lifetimes. It was like the loss of a very best friend not just once but ten thousand times. My client ached at the level of soul.

Once this pain was revealed to us, the relief was immense—I was able to see it and validate it. If this resonates with you as you're reading this, allow for the relief to come. There was *nothing* wrong with my client whatsoever. She wasn't having a breakdown, nor did she have a mental illness. She was grieving for a relationship that went so deep in her mind that she couldn't even begin to comprehend the loss. Relationships like this do not fit into our three-dimensional human mind's idea of normality. We are changing, we are evolving, and normality has to move and change with us. We feel things beyond this place in space and time. Honor this in yourself and in others.

A huge wave of healing came in for my client simply because she took the pressure off of herself to be what everyone wanted her to be, to grieve how everyone wanted her to grieve. Once that passed, we grounded ourselves and I taught her the following exercise, called "The Safe Release of Grief." It's not that you don't want to feel grief; you need to feel it to process and move through it. It's that you need a way to allow yourself to feel it without falling apart. You must feel it in manageable amounts so you know your life won't fall apart around you and feel it so you can release it, let go of that heaviness, and begin to feel like you can start to live your life again.

Exercise

The Safe Release of Grief

Make a space and time to do this, and give yourself twenty minutes afterward before resuming your daily activities. You can do the whole thing in an hour if you use thirty minutes for the exercise and thirty to lie down, daydream, or journal. So set an alarm for the first thirty minutes, and a second one for the latter. Put your phone in Airplane mode—silent just won't cut it. You need to go off the grid for this. You could also make space outside, sitting cross-legged on the grass, but remember that if you become emotional, you'll have to know how to handle it in a public place. And don't lie down in bed, because you'll fall asleep and won't do the work of it.

> Sit comfortably either in a chair or on the ground where your feet (or another part of your body) can comfortably touch the ground or earth below. Shoes off and barefoot if you're in a great deal of grief, otherwise flat shoes, slippers, or socks are fine.

> Bring your awareness fully into a space just above your head. If you have trouble doing that, you as the adult say out loud: "I am safe, I am here, I bring my awareness completely into this space." Using your will and intention to heal, allow more and more of your consciousness to arrive. If it helps, imagine yourself unhooking from what's at the forefront of your mind, whether it's something to do with work, dinner, or a family situation. Whatever it is will keep for an hour; you owe it to yourself to do your healing work. Say thank you to what keeps pulling your

awareness, and let it know that you'll be there for it in an hour or so when you've finished doing this.

As your awareness comes more into your body, bring your full awareness to the top of your head, and relax. Breathe out, feeling your feet on the ground. Tell yourself that you are going to release some of the grief you're carrying within. This exercise also works with shame, guilt, jealousy, dread, and fear, so you can adapt this exercise for any of these difficult, heavy emotions. The purpose is for you to tap into what you are carrying and release some of it as if you're decanting it from a barrel so you feel lighter.

Allow your body to show you where the barrel of grief resides in you. It's most likely to be in your stomach, but if it's bigger than your physical being, you can imagine it's there sitting beside you. How many of these barrels of emotional pain are you dragging around with you? Allow yourself to really feel grounded and safe, and then let yourself visualize a room of them. Depending on where you are with your healing work, you could see one or two massive barrels ... or just a few little ones.

No matter how many barrels there are, don't feel overwhelmed. Say thank you to the visualization and ask, "Is that all? Or is there more?" Let your image adjust until you can see just how much you are carrying today. And remember, you may only be showing yourself what you can handle; you may only be seeing one layer of it. And because this is called *safe release of grief*, that's exactly what we want to see.

Bring your awareness into your face, neck, shoulders, and upper chest. Use your slow breathing to bring yourself down, down into your body. Again, you can visit my website for an audio file of me doing this with you to help you get deeper and deeper into your body.

Get your bearings again with the visualization—has it shifted as you've become more grounded? Come into balance with it. Now start the release work. As you breathe out, you're decanting the liquid out of the barrel, and the barrel will shrink depending on how much you decant. Breathe in peace and calm; breathe out the emotion. Don't stop yourself from feeling it as you're breathing it out; the only thing you're not allowed to do here is step into victim mode, into "Why me? My life is so crap! It's just not fair" kind of talk. If you find yourself doing that, ask yourself which aspect of you is saying it and invite them to join you for the healing session. Let them watch as you use your will and self-control to breathe out the emotional pain. Let them cry with you or tell you what they need, or what you've missed by not consulting with them first. See this aspect of you as a friend; you're both grieving together.

Take lots of breaks. This exercise is not about breathing everything into nothing—it's about getting your bearings, finding out where you are with the unprocessed emotion, and being okay with it. It's about gently releasing some of that emotion and knowing that you can gently release it gradually, over time.

As long as you stay in your body and are purposefully breathing out the emotional pain gently, you're doing it right. In fact, if you have never been in your body, just coming in as far as you have is an achievement. Anything you willfully do in the direction of healing stimulates your body and soul to move in the direction of healing with you. Your goal is about bringing your whole self on the journey, so it will take time to get agreement from all the aspects of you. Remember also to stop when you've had enough. Just as with building muscle, you may not be able to do it for a full thirty minutes. In fact, it could take you those thirty minutes to come into your body. Make a date with yourself to do it again and notice if it doesn't take as long next time.

When you're finished breathing out the emotional pain, simply sit and breathe. Come into balance with the feeling of being lighter. Check the image of the barrels and see how it has shifted. Know that next time you do this (yes, you do need to do it more than once) you may have a different image depending on how much healing work has been going on in the background.

Give thanks to your body, soul, emotional self, and any aspect of you that showed up for the session. Stand up and take a stretch. Again, you may feel different in your body so get your bearings, check that you're grounded, and get yourself something to drink. Use your journal if you want to write down what came up for you, or go for a walk. Take that thirty minutes to embody what you did; it is so important. All this means is to allow yourself to feel the changes in your body. For those thirty minutes, just be with how you feel—don't try to do anything or engage with anyone, so you won't be pulled out of the healing. Know that you can do this; your life didn't end—you're okay. That in itself is such a gift.

A Few More Words on Grief

Just because you release grief doesn't mean you're no longer sad. You could be generating grief as quickly as you are releasing it, depending on the nature of what it is you have lost and where you are in your grieving process. Just be real with yourself. Be gentle—releasing grief like this does mean that the grief is still floating around in your system after the exercise has taken place. It could mean a stray wave of grief could catch you unawares as you're paying for the groceries or when you hear a song on the radio. Honor that. Find your feet. Connect to earth. Breathe. Steady the ship (so to speak), and use your breath to let it go, *gently*. Say to yourself, "This will pass and I will still be here. I am okay and it is safe to feel." Be that responsible adult riding the storm instead of the dramatic twenty-year-old stuck in the victim mentality or the abandoned child scared they'll never be loved again. With the work we are doing, please remember that you have an infinite source of love around you now. It's time to let yourself feel it.

Healing from a Breakup

A person's twenties are the most likely time to experience their first real relationship … and heartbreak. Some breakups are clean, a mature agreement by two people who have come to the realization that the relationship is not healthy for either party. But you're really not that mature in your twenties, so a breakup is more than likely to be messy and go on and on for months.

Issues That Come from Relationship Breakups

The biggest issue that people have when they come see me for help with a relationship breakup is that they feel they have not only lost a partner but they've lost a part of themselves too. It's as if the other person walked away and actually ripped off a part of them, leaving them bereft. This can happen energetically, and there are ways to heal. Grieving for a broken relationship can also be you grieving for a lost part of yourself.

If you've been the type of teenager who wore masks most of the time, allowing someone to see you as you really are can be exhilarating and terrifying. And when that someone, seeing you in all of your entirety, rejects you, the heartbreak also brings up major issues around self-esteem and self-worth. If this relates to you, again, there are ways to heal this—try the exercises below and know that your self-esteem will replenish itself over time as your heart heals.

There usually is a boundary line where we end and the other person begins; however, boundaries can be mixed when we allow someone to connect to us intimately. That's part of the elation when we fall in love, allowing that person inside so deeply. Some people find it difficult to repair their boundaries when a relationship ends; as if they've violated a sacred space you didn't even know existed and took your enthusiasm for life. In this situation, it can feel like you have no energy left to heal.

If you're already upset just reading these paragraphs, please try "The Safe Release of Grief" exercise earlier in this chapter around the loss of a relationship before you go further, because it is also a bereavement that needs to be honored and respected as such.

Know this: You don't *ever* have to make yourself stop loving someone. If your natural way to be is to love this person, no matter how much they hurt you, then be with that. Honor and respect yourself, build up your boundaries, and take as long as it takes to consciously protect what needs protecting, but don't ever force your heart to stop loving. The world needs more love. It's not a question about who deserves love and who doesn't depending on their behavior. Remember, we are all doing the best we can with what we know at the time, including that person you broke up with. It's possible that your soul recognizes their soul and loves them transcendent of space and time, no matter what their personality did or didn't do. Forcing yourself to stop loving someone is like cutting off a piece of you too.

Time to Heal

I love doing this work with people because when we are finished, the color comes back into their faces and they feel whole again and hopeful for the future. (Yes, this can be you too!) When clients come to me it's easy for them to know exactly which issue is bothering them because it's usually why they've come. For our purposes here, don't feel as though you need to drag up all the relationships you've ever had to do this work. Trust that your higher self will let you know.

Exercise

Reclaiming the Parts of You That Left When the Relationship Ended

Make a space for yourself to work where you won't be disturbed, and take as long as you need. Depending on the nature of the relationship, you might need to do this a few times over several days before the soul pieces you are receiving stay with you permanently. We have a tendency to drift back subconsciously. You might consider doing the work in part 2 of *How to Be Well*—how to heal the relationship with yourself and with other people, as you need to have a certain amount of personal power to be able to maintain the work done here.

Feel your feet on the ground, come into your body, and connect into the relationship breakup that you wish to heal. Imagine a cinema screen in your mind's eye, and allow the image of the ex-partner who took a piece of you when they left to appear on it. Depending on how you're feeling about this person today, you can visualize just their face in soft focus, or you can visualize their whole body. Come into balance with how you feel with them there. If there is excess emotion yet to be processed, let it come up.

Now with an open heart, say whatever it is you may need to say to this person, if you feel there is something left to say. Know that as you engage with the image of them in your mind, you're actually connecting into their energy, and they may feel it in this reality. Sometimes after doing this work clients have told me that their ex got in touch with them within hours of our session together, and some have even received text messages from the ex while in session. This is real work, so respect and honor it. Do not get angry with and make accusations at your ex—if that's what you want to do, go back and heal your wounded inner child or teenager. Only come to this work with peace and love.

Once you feel you have offered thanks for any lessons, apologies for past behavior, or forgiveness for hurting, make a space to let the energies settle. There is a transaction going on, and you may even get a sense of their side letting go, forgiveness, or even gratitude and love. Again, make space for emotions to come up if needed. This is amazing work, and the deeper you go into it, the more can be healed.

Before you disconnect with that person, ask their higher self (the part of them engaging with you) if they have any of your energy with them. Ask if you can please have your energy back so you can cleanly cut the cords of the relationship and move on with your life. It may be that they do have energy belonging to you or a part of your soul energy, but remember that you may also have soul energy belonging to that person in you. Perform an act of great generosity—allow yourself to reveal where in your body you may be holding on to that person's energy. Feel it as a texture or a density within you, or see it as a separate color. Notice if you're holding on to it and don't want to let it go—again be in grace and say thank you. Go heal that wounded abandoned child of yours. Or bring your wounded child along with you and say to it, "I will never abandon you. Right now, I need to let this go." Feel how your heart expands when you say those words to yourself, and allow yourself to open and release that energy. Feel it lifting up and out of you, and see a bright light healing and cleansing that energy before it goes through time and space along the pathway of your entanglement to the other person.

Ask again: "If you have any of my soul energy, please can I have it back now?" Wait and notice what happens. Feel your energy coming into the room where you are. When this happens, some people feel a sense of relief, great joy, and wholeness. Ask that this energy be cleansed and healed, and then allow it to gently merge with your body and soul, right here in space and time so that you feel like you've got that part of you back.

Next, offer great thanks to your ex-partner for taking part in this healing. Assure them that you've given them all of their essence, and then see that you have received all of yours in return. Ask for healing to come to you both to seal in that goodness, the beneficence of healing, so that you both are free to move on in your lives. You might imagine your ex-partner suddenly feeling happy, suddenly looking up and smiling and feeling as whole and new and as hopeful as you do in this moment. Allow yourselves to be wrapped in love. Then let the image of your ex-partner dissolve away, come back to the room, and come back to yourself.

Notes on Healing from a Broken Relationship

The process is usually (though not always) as straightforward as this exercise describes. If you're having difficulty with the release and the other party won't give you back your soul essence, you might need to get some help with it. Don't get angry, don't struggle—just dissolve it away and be with whatever it is. Then when you're ready, consider going to a spiritual healer or energy worker who can help you get your soul pieces back. In the appendix is a list of questions and things to think about before you book a session with someone new. (I am also available for this type of healing; my website is in the resources list.)

When I did this work with a friend of mine, his ex-girlfriend texted him thirteen (!) times during the session. I've often had clients forget to turn off their phone only to have it go off several times during work like this. Their ex-partner could feel the disturbance in the force field of the universe and could tell it was coming from their ex. This phenomenon proves again that energy work is real. So please do make sure you switch off all forms of contact while doing this exercise. And if your ex-partner does contact you, don't feel as though you must tell them what you have done. (You certainly can if you want, depending on the nature of your relationship and how things are between you now.)

Keep it all in the spirit of goodwill and make space for the possibility that their personality may be angry with you for releasing yourself. Energy work is not logical; we don't really understand how it all works. Remember that the work also takes place on a subconscious level—the other person is not knowingly and forcefully keeping a part of you hostage, it's just the way things are. Disconnecting from someone and reconnecting to yourself is so important, and it's all for the highest good of all. You, in turn, released the part of them you were holding on to as well…or did you? Maybe you need to take a few days to do the exercise again and go deeper with it. You, the responsible adult, will know what to do to make sure everything is healthy and good.

Embodying the Part of You That Came Home

Remember that as you sleep or become engaged in other tasks, the parts of your soul essence that came back during the reclamation exercise may drift back to your ex if you have low self-esteem or are still wounded in some way, shape, or form (and who isn't?). It could be that part of you feels you're not fully over the breakup or that things are not totally finished. It could also be that part of you feels you're unable to fully look after yourself. So you will have to repeat the exercise a few times over a few weeks to really feel the changes solidify.

If you have had a few breakups, I suggest against using the exercise with all your relationships all at once. Pick one ex-partner to work on first; choose the breakup that still hurts you the most. Stick with it and repeat the exercise a few times until you don't feel you need to anymore. And if you want to do the whole process again with another ex-partner, that's wonderful! Go for it when you've processed the first one.

To embody this work, you don't need to create a song and dance around it. Just look after yourself gently as you remember your worth. Notice the soul pieces coming back to you and see how much you've grown. They will remain with you with love and joy.

It is imperative that you, the responsible adult, give yourself what you need to get to that new healed place. You must look after yourself: eat well, sleep properly, stay away from things that make you ill or upset, and have fun on a regular basis. Have a daily spiritual practice to keep you connected into your heart. Trust yourself, believe in yourself, and you'll be there, for you.

How will you know when this piece of healing work is complete? Well, you won't need to ask yourself this question—you will feel it. You will wake up one day and feel more hopeful about life, more empowered to make changes, more inspired to be creative.

You will feel more confident and more contained in yourself. You will feel more whole, more present, and more able to enjoy life. You'll hear yourself laughing and realize that you're really, truly in the moment. And then you'll know.

Repairing Broken Boundaries

Once you reclaim the piece of yourself that left during a breakup, you will find you have enough energy to repair your boundaries. Big wounds require big energy to heal, so reclaiming energy from wherever you can is something I like to concentrate on first. If your boundaries were violated through violent acts, physical or emotional abuse, or something severely traumatic, the exercises are still effective and can still help you, but *please* make sure you have the support you need should a memory or a difficult emotion come up for you. You don't have to do this all by yourself.

What are boundaries, anyway? We are multidimensional beings, so it can be difficult to tell. How much of yourself do you give away to other people? There are many parts of you that you could give away; let's start with your time, your material possessions, your space, and your goodwill. You also give away your love, devotion, and soul essence.

Your soul essence is what we were reclaiming in the previous exercise, where two people fall in love, open their boundaries to each other, and mix together so they cannot tell what belongs to whom. After a breakup, it's messy, and new boundaries form but it's still not right energetically. Reclaiming your energy from them and giving back their energy brings you both into balance in a healthy way.

Energies can get mixed up between people in other ways too. If you were brought up in a family where they took your energy from you from the moment you were born, you may not know any other way of being. The pattern of expecting people will take your life force from you is at the level of the wounded child. Bring that child along with you the first time you do this just to make sure you don't leave any stone unturned.

Look for all the layers and levels that are impacted by boundary violation. Be patient with yourself. Keep a notebook and write down when you felt you should have said no and why, or when you realized that you gave away too much but it was too late already. You will need to educate yourself as to: (1) what you are doing, and (2) what you need to do instead. But if you don't do the energetic work you will be working from your mind alone, and the healing part won't be solidified. Do both parts together—mind and soul.

Exercise

Healing Your Energetic Boundaries

This is a visualization exercise, a bit like you sending a dream image made by your brain to your subconscious mind as an instruction, instead of having a dream sent by your subconscious mind to your brain for analysis.

You will, as with the other exercises in this book, need to repeat this so that the message gets through. Notice what behaviors are affected once the healing starts to solidify. You might find yourself more able to say no to things, to pull away from codependent patterns in a conscious way. And as with the other exercises, read it right the way through before you do it so that you know what to expect.

Make some time and space to sit and come into your body. Bring your awareness into the moment and into your heart. Take as long as you need to take to settle into yourself. You are going to step into a landscape where you can see your boundary as a wall/fence around you. Set your intention to learn about the current state that your energetic boundary is in so you can heal it. Each time you practice this exercise it will be different.

Visualize a field in open countryside. You are in the middle of this field; the field is you. Strewn around the field are big rocks and stones. There could also be rubbish in the field, abandoned litter, crashed cars… let the images reveal themselves to you as you sit in the center of the field. Each item represents something; the story behind it we don't really need to know, but you might know what it is. Either way is okay.

Notice if there is a boundary wall around you. The stones that make the boundary wall represent the strength of your boundaries. The diameter of the circle around you represents the amount of space you are taking up in the world. The clutter inside the boundary wall represents all the trauma you are holding inside of you that is related to your boundary issues.

Breathe with the boundary wall and let it come into form. This could be a very easy visualization for you to do, or it could be extremely difficult depending on where you are with your work. Just seeing the state of your boundaries and the amount of work that you need to do is enough for the first time you do this exercise. The wall will change by itself as you set your intention to heal. If you want to stop the work here, next time you will come back, try again, and go further with it.

By observing something it automatically changes. That's how energy healing works. We need to see it so we can heal it, so the change is in the direction of healing. As you settle with the images, allow them to shift and change as you let go of some of the things you have been holding on to. You can see yourself walking around, smashing up things that are too big, or just placing your hands on things that you wish to heal. As you do this, the things soften, grow smaller, or dissolve away.

Again, take your time with this; you may only wish to do some of this in one sitting.

Now work with the circumference of the circle. You don't need to drag stones around, but with the power of your intention and your imagination you can shift stones into place so that you have a better quality circle around you. Leave gaps between the stones if you want, or you can place them close together. Build a high wall if you feel you need to; pack it tightly and make it as thick as you feel you need, so you can be comfortable behind it. Sit in the center of the field, with the new boundary wall around you, and see what else you need to do with it. You might want to change the material of the stones to glass, to metal, to water. What would you like to use as your boundary substance? This is all temporary; as you heal, it will shift and change.

As you spend time with a stronger, more solid boundary wall around you, you may find that you're not taking up enough space in the world after all. Push out the wall so that the circle is larger, and notice how you feel when you do this. Stop when it feels like it's the right size for you.

Now let's work on the people inside your boundary wall. Choose someone you know is too deep in your energy field. Visualize them appearing inside the boundary wall. What are they doing? How are they behaving? Make sure that you are acting as your responsible adult self and talk to them. The conversation you have could sound like this: "Hello! I'm sorry that I've let you inside my boundary wall. Now it is time for me to heal myself and you're no longer allowed to come inside my field. Please, will you leave so that I can heal?" "Oh, I didn't realize! I will leave right away!" It would be great if it was always so simple, but sometimes negotiation is required; other times you can call on your angels or guides to act as a bouncer to gently but firmly remove them from the premises.

Once you have eliminated all the other people from your field, check the size of your boundaries again and see if there is anything else you want to do—change the density of the material again, or make the circle even that little bit bigger. Feel how your body feels. Allow yourself to feel spacious, powerful, strong. Let your self-esteem trickle in. Maybe as you do this you notice the land behind your boundary wall starts to flourish. Perhaps you want to plant trees and flowers, and turn it into a garden. This is your landscape, this is where you live, so do with it as you will.

When you finish this exercise be in grace and stillness. Allow the images to dissolve away and give thanks to your subconscious mind and your soul for working with you in this way. Notice how your body feels, how your heart feels, how your mind feels. Ask yourself what you need to do for you, to keep these changes in your daily life. And finally, say well done to yourself for doing something that you felt was difficult to do. It will get easier over time.

Bringing It All Together

By asking what you need to do for yourself at the end of this exercise to keep your boundaries strong and pure, you will receive information that you need to take seriously. Make a commitment to doing it, unless it isn't reasonable. Come to this exercise from a space of love, so when you are removing someone from your field you are doing it with love. Remember that the person is there subconsciously and may not even know they're doing it. And we are all here to learn from each other; if they had not "broken in" then you wouldn't have learned how to clear and heal your boundaries.

You can draw a picture of your field the way it looked when you ended the exercise. To reinforce it to your soul essence that it is not okay to let people come in and trash your energy field, solidify this image in your mind.

Hopefully as you get used to it, the changes you make during the exercise will solidify and stick, and you will come back to the images the way you left them. However, if the boundary you created while doing the exercise is totally obliterated since the last time you did it, then you need to look at your mind and your behaviors and see what it is that is allowing yourself to be violated. Just like you would program a GPS system to go from one place to another, imagine you are programming yourself to notice what it is that you do/say that gives the impression to other people that they can take from you. Don't change or fix anything, just become aware of things like how you're not able to say no to certain people, or what it is that has power over you. Again, there are empowerment exercises in *How to Be Well* that can help you reclaim your personal power and heal toxic dynamics in any relationship.

As you spend time with your boundary wall in your mind, it gets easier to flash up an image to see what is going on, and to sort it out there, in the energetic space. The results will trickle down into this reality and you'll be surprised how quickly you will see the results, once you are certain that you want to heal this. And if you don't, and are still being a victim, then your work may be with your inner teen, or your wounded child—go back to the Caregiver Child exercise and see if doing that again feels different once you have strong boundary walls in place. Ask yourself what you need to do to make this work stick with you and help you become the powerful creative being that you have the potential to be.

Ceremony to Honor the Work of Your Inner Twenty-Year-Old

When you do the work of healing aspects of yourself that were wounded, you consolidate your power, embody your presence, find it easier to move in the world, and choose joy and experience with an open heart. You may find that you need to stay here, in part 1 of this book, and go back and forth and back and forth to clear and heal the same things over and over again. But persist. How old are you in chronological years now? That is a lot of years to expect to be healed in the amount of time it takes to read this book. Do the work with joy and love. I have said this before: healing in the energetic doesn't take very long to show up in the physical. But you have to be in alignment with the work and you have to do it. It will take as long as it takes.

Ceremony is a wonderful way to mark the moment, to make real the work you have done. How would you like to celebrate where you have come from, the work that it took to get here, and where you are going to go to next? Write it down, and gift it to yourself.

Here are some ideas you could draw from, but thinking of your own is better as you're now the responsible adult stepping into the adult's shoes (may they be comfortable ones!) and so you have the power to decide what it is you want for yourself.

- Plant a tree/flowers in the garden to symbolize the new growth that you have worked toward.

- Burn/give away any material objects belonging to the person that you lost, write them a letter and burn it, light a candle, or burn incense, and release them completely from your energy field while allowing yourself to love them unconditionally.

- Visit a place where something happened in the past that upset you. Reclaim your power from that place and allow yourself to feel love and beauty there.

- Frame a photograph of yourself at the age where your core wounding happened that is now healed. Place flowers and a candle beside it. Honor the you that once was, and know that you are able to move on.

Affirmations

You can use affirmations to reinforce the work that we have done in this chapter. If you're feeling off balance and don't have time to go do one of the exercises again, or to sit in silence and let emotions pass through you, you can use an affirmation as an anchor to ground you in the present moment and remind yourself that you are safe, you are well, and you are loved. Here are some you can try. Just as before, notice how they sit with you in mind, heart, and instinct. There may be some work you need to do to clear any disbelief so that you can work toward believing each statement 100 percent.

- I am strong, I am safe, I can look after myself.

- I have good, strong, solid boundaries.

- I can release the heaviness of grief and not fall apart.

- It is safe for me to be with my difficult emotions.

- All of my energy is right here, with me, in this moment now.

- I allow myself to love whom I love without fear or regret.

- I am grateful for all of the experiences in my life.

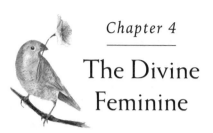

Chapter 4

The Divine Feminine

This chapter is about getting in touch with the feminine energies and healing the wounding that stems from there at any point in time in your life.

I am a woman and have experienced much of this wounding myself; I have also worked with many women clients and have facilitated and witnessed as they transformed their pain into joy. Therefore, this chapter is written from the point of view of the woman and I speak in terms of she; not he or it.

If you're a man reading this, know that you have these feminine energies inside of you too, and that we all are a balance of masculine and feminine. Read and allow your Divine Feminine aspect to become activated. Know that you may learn things about your mother, your sister, and all the women in your life, so read with an open mind. Know that you may also learn about yourself, so do not hesitate to try any or all of the exercises here with your inner "she." I urge all women to also read the next chapter, the Divine Masculine, just as I urge all male readers to continue to read this chapter, so we can understand the blends of the energies that we are all composed of, and learn how to balance them better.

We are all different: different cultures, different histories, different contracts, different blueprints to our souls. There are different blends within each individual too—the masculine woman, the feminine man; they are not out of balance, it's just the way the masculine and feminine have mixed within. No matter what sex your body is, no matter whether you're more feminine than masculine or the other way round, the key to healing anything is stripping away the lies and standing in the truth. We all thrive when we are authentic, both inside and out.

We stand here together, you and I, as the responsible adults that we are, always working toward balance. Know that we have aspects of ourselves that will show up and act out through us and need healing from us from time to time. We are learning how to recognize the child part of us when we throw a temper tantrum in a moment of weakness. Without judging ourselves, we are learning how to compassionately nurture that child part until it feels held, loved, and at ease. It is not that we will never trust anyone ever again but that the child in us is still learning to trust, and that trust begins with the relationship we have with ourselves.

So here we are, no longer a child, not in transition as a teenager going through the difficult stages of puberty where the body grows sometimes painfully in its shift from childhood to womanhood. Instead, we are now women, standing up to be counted. Somehow we still feel like a little child, even though we could be married, even if we have given birth to one or more babies.

The little girl in us still has not grown up. Why is that? Have we denied the years of puberty, of shifting and growth? And who are we becoming? With all the talk of feminism and women having to work harder in the world to get ahead, how are we supposed to hold ourselves?

When we lock away our Divine Feminine grace to make our way in the world of business, we become out of balance. When we hide in the bushes at night under the light of the moon to become the witch and cast spells on all those who have hurt or damaged us, we are out of balance. When the child aspect is the one who comes through most of the time, we are out of balance.

Divine feminine energies course through us but are only half of what we are, and we are at the same time learning what they mean, how to control them, and how to control ourselves. All of it must be honored. We need to learn what softness feels like...by allowing ourselves to be soft. We need to acknowledge that beauty exists, and allow beauty into our lives. We can be graceful and dance and flow with curves and smoothness, we can be the comfort that is missing from our own lives. What does being a woman really mean? What wounding has prevented us from being in the flow of our divine birthright?

Becoming a Woman: The Passage from Girlhood to Womanhood

In most of Europe and America, we do not celebrate the passage into womanhood. There is no official initiation ceremony. We have noticed the lack, and through the work of red tents, women's circles, and support groups, it's becoming more talked about and more acknowledged that it is needed. If we could step from girlhood into womanhood in community with everyone as witness, where mothers would look upon their daughters as the women that they are becoming, where daughters could step into the role of woman and believe their voice is important, many of the problems we have as women would disappear.

I have clients who are in their late forties and fifties with mothers who are in their seventies and eighties. My clients still think of themselves as little girls, even when they have little girls of their own. This does not bode well for the youngest generation. If you are reading this and are a mother—even if your own mother is still alive—you must endeavor to prevent the mother-daughter wounding from passing down to your daughters. Remember that *you* are the mother. Your mother is the grandmother. Reclaim your power. And feel safe and secure enough in that power so that you can give your daughter her power too.

When you see your mother as the woman she is instead of a goddess who birthed you and is perfect and complete, it enables you to step into womanhood and motherhood too. The fear of making a mistake dissolves because you recognize the mistakes your own mother has made. It opens the horizon for you to be who you are and take on the role without having to become your mother in the process. We need to honor the women who gave birth to us in all of their imperfections and release them from our need for them to be perfect mothers. Embrace Mother Earth as your mother instead, for she is the one who can love you unconditionally, where a human being with their fixed ideas, their character, and personality is unable to do so.

Accepting your mother for who she is completely as a person—flaws and all—means that you and your mother can then become two women together—clean, clear, equals, friends, and (hopefully) generous people with open hearts. You no longer need to lean on her or cut off pieces of yourself to please her, or lose yourself completely in her to be her support. This realization of freedom can heal the victim mentality that travels throughout the female lineage across all cultures. By doing the work in this book, you can heal your abandoned inner child knowing that you will never abandon yourself, and thus you won't be a victim. Now it's time to free yourself as a woman too.

As well as the lack of ceremony that keeps us from our natural growth, we are now afraid of aging due to media and pressure from consumerism—botox and cosmetic surgery are more popular than ever to "keep us young." Grandmothers will not claim their position as elders but instead want to stay mothers for as long as they can. Using products to eliminate wrinkles, wearing younger fashions, and taking up yoga do not make one chronologically younger. Aging is a part of life, and it needs to be embraced. It is time for grandmothers to be grandmothers, for mothers to be mothers, and for daughters to have the space they need to grow into the mothers they could become.

Exercise

Journaling

Where do you sit with this work? Here are some questions I've created so you can get a reading on your emotional body, your mental body, and your spirit.

- Do you have a mother wound? If so, can you name what it is?

- What aspect of you has been impacted the most by your mother wound? Have you healed it with the work you've done so far in the book or do you need to do more?

- What is the dynamic between you and your mother now, as adults?

- Do you feel like a grown woman, or are you still acting out of your child?

Remember, you must be authentic and clear in yourself when you do these exercises—if not, you're kidding nobody but yourself. And when you hide something from yourself, you cannot heal it. Here's your opportunity to go deep to release the pressure you're putting on yourself. It links nicely with the "Becoming Your True Self" exercise in chapter 2.

More questions for you to contemplate:

- What does being a woman mean to you?

- What does being a mother mean to you?

- Did you expect your mother to be something she is not?

- What was it?

- How can you heal this?

I'm not saying that we all have a mother wound; if you don't feel you do, that's wonderful. Keep reading, because we will cover quite a bit of ground you may find relevant to you. If your mother wound is the biggest you've received, go gently with this. As usual, I ask you to have support around you if you choose to do the work in this book, someone who you trust who can witness you releasing the pain and reclaiming who you are.

Preparation Work

When our boundaries bleed into each other, it's difficult to tell ourselves apart from the other. The mother work is of separation, love, respect, and the recreation of boundaries. The healing comes when you can see the other as a person in their own right, and see yourself as that too.

In order to claim yourself as woman, there are a few things that must be done in preparation. You must disconnect the energetic cords and binds between you and your mother. You must reclaim your power from any past relationship. You must also heal your inner wounded child.

Limiting Beliefs about Your Mother

Do you feel your mother is capable of looking after herself? Who is the mother—you or her? Your thought patterns dictate the energetics of this relationship. If you're feeling she needs you, then you're offering yourself to her and setting up the energy so that she will take as much as she wants from you. Don't get me wrong: if she is physically ill and needs you to help her, there still is a difference between two adults helping one another and a grown woman being treated like a child.

Exercise

You Are Not Your Mother

This exercise is to help you firm up in your mind the idea that your life is not your mother's life, you are not your mother—

you are you. Even if you have similar tastes, you're both different people. Knowing this at the subconscious level can take a while to achieve.

Take each statement here and think about it, write about it. Take a day or longer with each one so you embody it.

- I am not my mother, I am myself.

- I am living my life, I am not living her life.

- My mother is a capable adult who has made her own decisions. I do not owe her anything.

- I make my own choices, and I give her the freedom to make her own choices.

- My mother and I do not have to agree on everything.

- I will not go against my own heart just to spite my mother.

When we feel our mother has let us down, the anger we fee toward her can sabotage our own lives. I had a client who loved pottery. Her mother also loved pottery, so my client gave up pottery because she didn't want to have any similarity to her mother. Learning that she could love pottery in her own right and that she could do the things that she loves without turning into her mother was a huge revelation for her. Can you relate to this?

Know that if you want your mother to accept you as you are, you also need to accept her as she is. It is an important step for you to clarify this so take as long as you need.

You can revisit the "Reevaluate Your Values" exercise in chapter 2 to help you do this, work with your caregiver child from chapter 1, or take all of this to a therapist and have them help you work through it. Ask the question, "What will it take for me to claim my rightful place as a woman in the world?"

Disconnecting from Your Mother at the Energetic Level

This exercise is similar to reclaiming your power from an ex-partner. You will need to repeat this many times before the energies settle, depending on the relationship you have with your mother. Even if you feel it's a good relationship and you're respected as a woman, this exercise is still very healthy to do and I recommend you do it no matter what state your relationship is in. If you have a stepmother, then do it with your birth mother and with your stepmother. If you were brought up by your grandmother, do it with her and your birth mother. You cannot overdo this particular exercise. Even if you never met the woman who gave birth to you, or your mother has died, you can still cut the ties between you both, because you are connected to each other in the energetic realms.

Exercise

Disconnecting from Your Mother Energetically

Make a quiet space for yourself. Notice how you are feeling about doing this exercise. Know that you may feel physical pain during or after the exercise. Know that your mother may feel the results of this exercise and contact you or act out of her own inner child as you disconnect from her. Know also that all of these energetic cords are the result of natural things we do at a subconscious energetic level; nobody is "feeding" off of anyone on purpose. Just decide that it's time for you to step out of your mother's energy field, create stronger boundaries, disconnect all ties, and see yourself as a complete human being in your own right. Be with the idea of this and how it makes you feel. Limiting beliefs may show up, such as "I can't do this" or "If I disconnect from her, I'll hurt her." You can do this, and you won't hurt her. It's healthier to cut the cords. If you want to go deeper with this, check out my book *How to Be Well*.

Visualize your mother in your mind's eye. Notice how your energy feels when you do this. Allow the image to get stronger. See your mother in a bubble of light; see yourself in a bubble too. Then visualize the cords that connect the two of you together. Sometimes when I do this some of my clients cannot tell the difference between their energy and their mother's energy. If that's the case, choose to be one color and make her another. Some clients feel as though their bubble is inside of their mother's bubble, and that's okay too. Just allow yourself to see it however it presents itself to you. The first time is always the most difficult. There can also be energy cords binding you both to each other, and it is possible that your daughter cords are more strongly connected to your mother's energy than your mother is connected to you, depending on the soul contract and the relationship between you both.

Say out loud: "I am now disconnecting completely from my mother's energy." Notice if simply saying this causes you anxiety—if so, that's okay; it's part of the process and might take you longer, so go gently. If you wish, say her name or change the words. Visualize the two bubbles, yours and your mother's, shifting and loosening so that there is more space between you. Breathe and be slow while you do this, and notice how your body feels. Bring the two bubbles up to the same level in your mind's eye so they are on an equal plane. See these two adults together, of equal value. Allow your energy to expand so that your bubble gets bigger, stronger, and brighter. Let your mother's bubble do the same so she has more space. You are not subservient to her energetically. How does your body feel now?

Finally, allow for the energy cords between you both to dissolve away. Release each other so you are no longer feeding into her bubble of energy and she is no longer feeding from yours. Feel how buoyant you become when the cords are dissolved and disconnected. Feel the joy coming into the space between you as you claim your right as an adult. End this exercise by saying thank you to your mother for the lessons she has taught you.

A New Level of Relationship with Your Mother Is Possible in This Physical Reality

If you want to stay in a relationship with your mother, feel the difference now, as it has changed to a new level where you are equals. What I mean by this is simple: you no longer have to mind your mother if that's what you have been doing in the past. Allow for that knowledge to trickle into the conversations and behavior you both act out of. See her for the woman that she is, totally capable as an adult. Be there to help her when she needs help but know that you're not responsible for her anymore. The same goes the other way as well—you don't have to be roped into anything or do anything because you feel you have to. You can do it because you *want* to.

Once you are aware of your relationship with your mother and continue to work at the energetic level to heal it, your mother can no longer drain your life force. You now know that to ensure she's not draining you, you can repeat this exercise as often as needed until you train yourself to not connect to each other the same way again.

Connecting to Mother Earth as the Mother Who Can Hold You Unconditionally

Once you have released your mother to be the woman she is in all of her imperfections, it allows you to become the woman *you* are in all of your imperfections too. Feel the brightness and the freedom; imagine yourself on a mountaintop with all the world beneath you. You can send energetic roots down through the mountain, feeling its strength holding you, as you feel safe enough to open yourself out fully. Unzip yourself, expand your energy, and feel the joy of simply being.

As humans, we tend to shrink and take up less space energetically in the world rather than be at our full size, so expanding and spreading energetically take work and practice. Try what I have just said as a visualization when you are relaxed in a quiet moment. It can be very powerful. Try it every day for a week and each day it will feel stronger, different, more substantial. Notice what happens in your day that simply flows, what you're able to forgive, walk away from, and not get upset about where you would be upset under normal circumstances.

Next, notice what makes you small again, when you shrink back into the wounded child, the lost and ungrounded human, the small you who needs to be held. If you realize what is happening, then you as the responsible adult can do something about it rather than just give into it.

So go to that actual mountaintop, and do this work on the land. Or go to the beach, and feel the expanse of the horizon and the wildness of the sea, the pure potential, as the energy holds you so you feel safe enough to open fully. Feel accepted, flaws and all. Feel the beauty in nature reflected back in your ability to feel safe, and to ground yourself in it. Be grateful from the bottom of your heart, and let go of your internal battle to be good enough. You are good enough already. Just allow yourself to be who you are in all of your fullness, and let Mother Earth be the mother that you were always looking for.

Ceremony to Connect to Mother Earth

There is no better way to connect to earth than to go outside and set your intention to connect. You can do this in your garden or front lawn, or visit a landmark, sacred site, or somewhere that means something to you. Next, make plans to visit. Look into whether you need to book tickets, if it's public or protected, and if you can expect some quiet and sacred time there. Nothing's worse than deciding to go somewhere only to find out it's not what you thought it was.

Bring something that you can use as an offering—food, flowers, or anything else that is biodegradable. Please don't bring pictures, ribbons, or anything with plastic in it, because it's no longer an offering, it's litter. When I do this I usually bring cut flowers, chocolate, or alcohol. Also make sure you're wearing appropriate clothing and are going at an appropriate time of day (e.g., when the tide is out or before dark). Bring a rubbish bag and gloves with you too; if you have a car, these are good things to always have whenever you travel. It always amazes me how disrespectful people can be; if you want, it could be your offering to the land to clean up the sacred space before beginning the ceremony.

When you get to your destination, bring your offering with you. Approach your chosen site in silence. Be grateful in your mind, graceful in your step, and leave no trace of your visit behind you. At the entrance to where you have chosen to visit, stop and be in reverence. Ask permission to connect to the energies there. Wait for an answer. When you receive a yes, give thanks and enter with solemnity. Find a spot where you feel safe. Sit and connect to your heart. Then connect through your body to the earth beneath you.

You can say a prayer in your mind or speak it out loud. You can talk to the land and tell her all of your worries, your pain. You can allow the emotion to well up inside you and then give it to the land. Allow her to take it from you. Embrace the idea that the land can hold you no matter what you have done, where you have been, or how long it has been since you connected. Offer your tears to her, your laughter.

Give thanks, sing a song, make your offering. Let the joy come in, and let it shine out through you into the earth. Feel held. Feel seen. Let the earth spirits come to you and show you a sign. If you are still sitting, rise. Make a wish for you, and a wish for the land. Feel the land energy flowing through you, see the land in your heart. When you're ready to leave, stop once more at the entrance, turn and face the place where you were, and give thanks again. Walk away feeling lighter, more connected to joy, and with the knowledge that the earth holds you, and that Mother Earth loves you, no matter what.

The beauty of doing this is that when you're feeling upset or small, you can call on these places that are now instilled in your heart and mind to reconnect to those energies that held you. You can once again feel them comforting you, even when your body is not physically there. Over time, that comfort and knowledge will become naturally embodied within you because the more often you do it in reality, the easier it becomes to go there energetically. I highly recommend this ceremony and recommend it be done often in different places so you start to feel like you are of the land—you *are*, because you are alive.

Reclaiming Your Body: Sacred Intimacy

It's difficult to put the wounding of the Divine Feminine into a simple frame because there are so many facets to it. Body loathing, body shaming, and body image are all wounds inherited and cultural; we all have a wound of rejecting the female body … your body. In essence, you have been told through the media that your body is not good enough as it is because it's too fat, too skinny, too small, too tall, too round … It was bullying in the schoolyard, side comments in the galleries. And like most other women in Western society, you have more than likely grown to hate your body because of this. You possibly inherited your attitude toward your body from your mother—perhaps as a girl you noticed her attitude when she saw herself in the mirror, saw her trying on clothes, changing her mind and not being happy with anything she wore. Maybe she was constantly on a diet and often criticized her own body…and possibly yours too. In essence, this type of wound is still part of the mother wound.

Another aspect of mother wounding affecting the body is some mothers' inability to bear that their children may be prettier than them, resulting in them wanting to take the light away. These mothers put their daughters down to ensure they are not noticed. Many mothers of clients of mine have seen their daughter as more beautiful than them and resent them for it. As a result they are overly critical of their daughters, feed them too much so they put on weight, and tell them they will never amount to much. Some of this is shadow work, which will be explored in chapter 6. In cases like this, the mother's shadow is activating the daughter's, but let's do this work first. Know that if you have terrible difficulty with mother wounding, there is shadow work as well as some inner child work to be done. Marry the work together so it is all done in tandem. Take your time, as this type of wound does not heal quickly. Know that if you can heal this, as the mother or as the woman, you heal it for your daughters, your granddaughters, and your great-granddaughters. You can see that it's worth putting in the effort.

Here are some examples of how the mother wound can affect the intimate relationship we have with our own body:

"I hate my body…it's so fat, I carry around so much fat I wish I could just cut it off with a knife. I might die from doing that but I don't care. I'd rather die than look like this."

"I can't make love to my boyfriend because I'm too embarrassed to be naked in front of him. I make sure the room is dark, let him do what he wants, and fake my orgasm so that it's over really quickly."

"I had a baby and now I hate my stretch marks, I hate my loose, saggy tummy. I'm so unhappy with how I look."

"I can't go dancing tomorrow night, I've got the curse. What's the curse? Oh, it's my period. I hate it, all the blood. I wish I wasn't born a woman."

All of this hating of our bodies is absorbed by our bodies, and our bodies get heavy with the hate. Just as we have wounded child aspects and inner teen aspects, our body is also an aspect of us. If we hate our bodies, we are actively hating a part of ourselves, and that creates disconnection. When we cut ourselves off from our bodies, we cannot feel our feelings and lose our greatest resource—our inner wisdom.

Exercise

Journaling

Think about this:

- If you totally accepted your body in all of its glory, how would your life be different?
- What type of clothing would you wear?
- What would you do that you're not doing?
- What would you not do that you are doing?
- How would your attitude toward other people's bodies change?

If you're the type who criticizes other people based on how they look, then you are most certainly your own worst enemy because you are projecting your own imperfections outward to others so you can feel better about yourself. The core issue, then, is that you don't feel good about yourself. Truly, who cares what other people look like? Leave them to it!

Do you want to heal this in you so your children can heal? To break the chains of ancestral pain around body image and body shaming is a big undertaking, and it is so important. Let me say this before you skip to the next section: if you don't do it, you are not accepting a part of yourself and cannot ever become whole. Healing all of the aspects of yourself includes healing your relationship to your body. It can take years to do, so read with an open mind, see where you are with yourself, and try some of the exercises. And again, get help if you need help.

You don't need to dress up and take a goddess workshop, dance under the moonlight, cast spells using your menstrual blood, or take all of your clothes off in front of other people. You don't have to do any of these things to accept your body in its fullness. I don't do any of those things, as they don't resonate with me. But if you want to do them, that's fine too! Someone who ran a café in Glastonbury, UK, said to me that the people who constantly treated her waitresses badly were participants in the goddess workshops. So if you do want to do anything like this, do it authentically; be truly who you are, with your whole heart, rather than using it as an excuse to put on another mask and hide from your real work.

What I think you need to do most of all is slow down. Allow your awareness to come completely into your body. Feel what you are feeling and breathe it out. Be fully present to each body part. Ask forgiveness for what you demand of it, for what you expect it to do for you that it can't. Pay special attention to your stomach and womb. Sacred intimacy is what I'm talking about here, and I offer you some work to do to grow into having a more sacred and more intimate relationship with your body. *Sacred* here means instilling a feeling of reverence, appreciation, honor; "intimacy" here refers to closeness, connection, and union.

Healing the Relationship with Your Body

I am writing three exercises here you can do to relax in, forgive, and become more connected to your body. Depending on where you are with yourself, each one could be a challenge for you, or one of these exercises may be more of a challenge than others. All are simple in one respect and the hardest in another. They build upon each other (you need to do the first one first), and becoming comfortable with the first one makes the second one easier, and then the third. Do them in order, and break each one up into small parts until you can do the whole thing in one sitting. Take your time—your body isn't going anywhere.

Exercise

It Is Safe to Relax

It's so important for this exercise that you make a space where you won't be disturbed. Make the effort to create a space that is comfortable and warm, as nice as if a friend were coming over. But this is for you, so create a space to honor your sacred self. Have fun with it. Play nice music, have nice scents—you can even do this in a bath with candles all around you and dim the lights to feel safe. If you are serious about the work, you will need to create this space often, so don't go crazy with making a once-off amazing space. Make a space that is safe to which you can come back again and again easily.

Before you start, make sure the phone is off, that you won't be disturbed for at least thirty minutes. As you start to prepare yourself for the work, ask yourself, "Do I feel safe here?" If not, figure out what's in the way of your feeling completely safe and sort that out. Write down everything in your mind that will not let you be at peace for the next thirty minutes. Once it's out of your head and on paper, you won't have to go over the same thoughts again and again. Now you can allow yourself to relax and do your work. Only go as far as you're able in one sitting. Keep going with this until you're able to relax your whole body.

Breathe and slow down. Say out loud, "I am safe, I feel completely safe here." Get a reading on yourself, make sure the statement is true, and if it isn't, find out why and then see what you can do to fix it. For example: "I am feeling 80 percent safe, so there's a part of me that doesn't feel safe. Which aspect of me is it, and what do they need so that they feel safe to relax?" Know that your mind can make up reasons to not feel safe and sometimes your energy can pick up reasons to not feel safe from other people—it's all perfectly natural. Lock into your feeling of fear and breathe it out. Feel your feet on the ground and know that logically everything is okay.

Another helpful and effective method to get into this space is to phone or text a friend and ask them to hold you in a space of safety for thirty minutes so you can feel more at ease. Feeling your friend's energy around you can help you feel held enough so you can relax and go deeper. Holding space for you means that your friend has you in their thoughts and they visualize you being safe, relaxed, and feeling good for the period of time you specify. After the thirty minutes are up—and this is so important—they let you go, as they cannot hold this space for you indefinitely because it takes energy. You can do this for them too, and probably already have; in times when your friend was doing something difficult, you may have held them in your thoughts as being able to do it and visualized them doing it with ease and grace.

Next in our work are mindful breathing, controlled focus, and awareness. Your mind needs to be doing this alone and nothing else, so keep bringing it back to your body if it wanders. Allow the relaxation to come in, and let go of the burden of stress you are carrying. Our bodies carry more stress than we realize, so no matter how relaxed you think you are, there is always more stress to release. It might be really difficult to do this, hence my suggestion to be in a hot bath, as the water can help ease the strain of the tension too.

> Feel your awareness coming more and more into the room where you are. Feel your energy settle down and feel your body relax as you become even more aware of your surroundings, of your body, of how you are feeling. Become aware of your breathing and slow it down.

> "I feel safe, it is safe for me to relax." Say this statement several times, breathe out whatever rises in you that isn't sure about whether or not it feels safe. The more often you try this, the easier it becomes. Feel your feet on the ground, feel Mother Earth beneath you. Breathe out the

fear and become closer to truly feeling 100 percent safe, or as safe as you can be.

With every exhale, bring your awareness deeper into your body, bring the idea of being relaxed into your muscles, your bones, your nervous system. You can do this for the whole body to start with, giving your body permission to relax, because you are truly safe. Remember to not judge any body part—all body parts are treated equally in your mind during this exercise.

Now we close in on the body in more detail. Focus your awareness on your mind, on the top of your head, and on your face. Say, "I feel safe, it is safe for me to relax," and as you breathe out, feel all the tension leaving your mind, your brain, your face. Know that you've written down those thoughts of yours, so if your mind interrupts the process, you can remind it that you've got those thoughts and you don't need to go over them again. Let your face soften, feel your mind release, and notice how tight you hold that part of yourself. Spend at least five breaths here, slowing down, releasing tension, relaxing.

Move your awareness down to your neck, shoulders, and upper chest. Breathe in, "I feel safe, it is safe for me to relax," and breathe out the tension. Really feel what it is like to be in your body, to feel safe, to relax. Stay with the chest until you feel your shoulders drop and your breathing deepen. You can also imagine bindings around your chest loosening, like you're taking off a tight corset or bra. Let waves of stress and tension leave your body and as that happens, you show up, you allow yourself to be fully who you are. You don't have to hold it in; it is safe to relax. Spend at least five deep breaths here, slowing down, releasing tension, relaxing.

Move downward now to your heart, lungs, and upper and middle back. Say the statement again: "I feel safe, it is safe for me to relax." At this point you might want to yawn, stretch, and tense and release your muscles. Go ahead. Speak to your chest when you say those words, allow your body to expand, and your energy will also expand. Spend some time with your heart; check in and see how it feels. You might like to do some of the heart work we did in chapter 3 on healing a broken heart just to bring healing and relief to your heart. Your heart can shut down just from day-to-day life; it's always good to do healing work. Spend at least eight very slow, deep breaths here, slowing down, releasing tension, relaxing.

When you do this work, don't be in a rush. If you are already at the thirty-minute mark, then stop here and come back and do the whole thing again another time (yes, start from the beginning) or if you feel like you want to continue, then keep working.

Move downward again, to your stomach and lower back. Breathe in and out, releasing all the muscles and relaxing your body, and say out loud, "I feel safe, it is safe for me to relax." This can be difficult as we hold our stomach in so tight. Listen to what your stomach may want to say to you, as you let it relax and release—ask it if there's anything you can do to help it come into balance. Your stomach holds guilt, anger, fear, frustration, shame … It also is affected by the foods you eat and is always processing either food or emotion. So it's a complex, busy area. Spend at least ten slow, deep breaths here. Go deep in, relax the muscles, and really feel into your stomach area with your awareness and your attention.

Move your awareness into your hips now. Feel the stability of your pelvis, bring your awareness into your root area, between your legs—your anus, your genitals. Isn't there such a lot of wounding here? Even as I write, referring to this area is difficult; it's a delicate matter. How can we discuss this area without the sting of emotional energy around it? Bring your awareness here and sit with your nether regions. Say, "I feel safe, it is safe for me to relax" and do your best to let go of any shame that you are carrying for any reason. As you relax the tension here, you might need to bring your responsible adult in to reassure yourself that you're beautiful and natural, that you're allowed to be a sexual being, that you excrete as part of your body's natural processes. This is all part of being alive, and if you're holding emotional pain around your bowels, genitals, womb, root area, there is work to do. Just gently acknowledge it, know that it's there, sense a simple awareness of it; sense that it can awaken a release, a knowledge and a knowing in you of what you need to do to heal it. It's a wounding, a mother wounding, maybe from giving birth, from something someone said to you, or from a cultural requirement. Let it reveal itself to be healed without you needing to fix or change anything right now. Just breathe with it, be with it with love in your heart if you can. Let any emotions move through you. Stay here for as long as you can, at least eight long, slow, deep breaths. When you feel ready to, you can then move on. And if you have released big emotion it is important to keep going so you can ground yourself, to create that conduit to earth so you can continue to release the emotion and give it to Mother Earth.

Bring your awareness to your legs. Relax the muscles in your legs, your knees, your lower legs, right to your ankles. If this is too much, relax the upper legs to the knee first, then go to the lower part to the ankles. Say out loud, "I am safe, it is safe for me to relax." Notice how it feels to say it, and again, if you're not feeling safe, ask yourself what is going on, and what you can do to heal this. Imagine your muscles are melting and falling off the bones of your legs; the deeper you relax the softer you are becoming. Stay in your legs for at least five slow, deep breaths and notice how much more relaxed you feel for doing it.

Moving down to your ankles and feet, say to them, "I am safe, it is safe to relax" and feel the power that your feet bring; visualize them growing cords of light and connecting to the earth, going deeper and deeper as you get stronger and stronger. Make sure these cords of light are big enough so that you feel like you're really connecting your whole body deep into the heart of Mother Earth.

Remembering the work we already did with Mother Earth, remind yourself that Mother Earth can hold you, nourish you, and be the one who cherishes you where perhaps your own mother didn't do that for you. Now bring your awareness to the whole of your body—know that you've got inner wounding from being alive, that you've still got stress and tension deep in your muscles, tissues, and bones. Know that you have scars on your body from being alive, that what you have is not the body your mind may say you want but it's *your* body, the one that you have right now, today, in this moment—and it is doing its best for you. Tell your body that you're totally safe, connected to Mother Earth, and that everything is as it should be. See how you feel now.

Big work. Well done, truly. Even just reading this is big work. When you do, it's like unlocking a door that has been closed inside you for years. Perhaps you've discovered a messy room, but that room is full of treasures to be discovered. It's a room you don't want to abandon ever again.

Forgiving Your Body for Not Being What You Want It to Be

If you have been able to do the "It is Safe to Relax" exercise in its entirety and opened up that room that is full of treasures inside you, this exercise becomes much, much easier.

To make this exercise even more effective you can do some groundwork. Do the "It is safe to relax" exercise a few times, let the different parts of your body speak to you and tell you why they don't feel safe. You might be surprised—your body may not feel safe from your criticism and your fixed ideas of what your body should be, compared to what your body actually is.

Your mind is the one that needs educating here, so look online and find YouTube videos about how magazines edit images to the extent that models in magazines don't look like real bodies. Tell yourself that your fixed ideas around what is beautiful are what is at fault here, not your body. I highly recommend watching *Embrace*, a 2016 movie by Australian photographer Taryn Brumfitt who goes around the world and meets women who hate their bodies in all different cultures because they don't look the way they want them to look. She says, "We are not fat, we *have* fat, just like we are not fingernails, we *have* fingernails." It's a different way of framing it and really changes the energetics around how you see your body and yourself. It's a wonderful movie, and I highly recommend it. Your body will thank you for it.

Know that your body looks the way it looks because of your genetics, your environment, and what you have been feeding it. When I say "feeding," I mean food, drink, and substances like medicines and other such chemicals. But I also mean your thoughts, what you read/watch/listen to most of the time, and the people you spend most of your time with, as all of these things create the energy that your body absorbs, like a sponge. Know that your body looks the way that it looks because of how you have been exercising or not exercising it. If you're not happy with your body, that is totally okay, really it is. And you can change it! You must realize, though, that it's not your body's fault, and it's time to forgive your body and work with it instead of constantly fighting against it.

If you're battling this idea and are really resistant to doing this part of the work, I suggest going back to chapter 2 to do the Becoming Your True Self exercise about your body. You're the responsible adult now, so it's time to stop kidding yourself—you won't have an athletic body if you eat pizza and don't exercise. For now, the part I want to heal with you is the anger and frustration you have with your body for not being athletic when you eat pizza and don't exercise. That's the nonlogical part. I honestly don't care if you eat pizza every day and don't exercise ... but I do care if you blame your body for it!

Another thing you might not be aware of is that if you spend time actively hating your body, you're bombarding it with anger and resentment, which solidifies into heavy energy you carry around with you. Just like fat, it weighs you down, and it takes extra energy to carry it around. If you stop actively hating your body, and forgive it for being what it is and ask it to forgive you for being so mean to it, you neutralize a cycle of heaviness, which, in turn, gives you a burst of energy back. That's the energy you need to give you the motivation to get off the chair and shop for some good, nutritious food and learn how to cook it, or to go to the gym and do the workout that you're complaining that you have no energy to do.

If you have not resolved how you feel about your body, my suggestions won't really work. And if your self-saboteur is determined to destroy everything you create, then perhaps you need to marry this with some of the shadow work we will do in chapter 6. Learn about yourself; observe how you are with this instead of walking away and giving up. If these acts of forgiveness are so difficult for you, then it's work you need to do, and you may need additional support to do it. Go back to heal your inner teenage wounding about not fitting into the crowd. Heal your broken heart and tell yourself that whatever did or didn't happen in your life wasn't because of your body, it was because of your attitude toward yourself and your low self-esteem. There are plenty of highly successful people out there with bodies that don't work as well as yours does; my favorite quote about this is from Sargent Johnny Joey Jones: "People ask me how I can stay so positive after losing my legs…I simply ask how they stay so negative with theirs."

Exercise

Forgiveness Ritual for Your Body

A ritual is something that you do often; how often is up to you. If you berate your body frequently about how it doesn't look the way you want it to look, how it underperforms for you, then doing forgiveness as a ritual is a way for you to balance this, until it becomes embodied for you and you stop needing to do it because you no longer berate yourself. That's the goal, anyway.

I love the Hawaiian prayer *Ho'oponopono,* and it makes a wonderful basis for a forgiveness ritual. It goes like this:

> *I'm sorry*
> *Please forgive me*
> *Thank you*
> *I love you*

You're going to say these words to your body, and if you want context around it, you can say: "I'm sorry for being so mean to you. Please forgive me for not appreciating you as you are and wanting you to be something else. Thank you so much for still being here, for not giving up on me."

Now comes the hard part. "I love you" might be too difficult for you to say to your body. What do you want to say instead? How about something like "I'm here for you now, I see you in the pain that you're in because of me, I promise to do better, I appreciate you more than I realize."

You get the drift—whatever you say, you have to mean it. The beauty of this prayer is that the energy is in the words, so you don't need to add anything else. Just the four simple lines above are more than enough to heal this if said often enough and with meaning.

Next is the ritual, which may also be a challenge for you. Come into your body like we did in the "It is Safe to Relax" exercise. When you focus on a body part, say this prayer to it, over and over again with every breath. Building on the work we have already done, you are now infusing your body with healing and love. Every single part of your body will feel it, especially the parts you dislike. This powerful prayer carries with it a loving, healing energy. And because you've been putting a nasty, harsh energy into your body (particularly to the parts you dislike), it's time to heal them. You don't need to put context around every body part; in fact, you don't need to put any context around this prayer at all. Just say the words to your face, "I'm sorry. Please forgive me. Thank you. I love you." Say them a few times but for this to work, you *must* mean them. Your body knows when you're lying, and so do you. So just as you figured out why you didn't feel safe and fixed it as best as you could, you must now clear the gap between what you believe and what you're saying. The beauty of this is that it's not the responsible adult part who doesn't believe you... it's usually the wounded child part. Figure it out, and then go heal the child. Bring the child along with you when you say this prayer to your body parts. Here's an example of how that could work.

To your inner six-year-old: "Your face isn't horrible, it's your face. It's the only one you have, and it's doing a great job. That girl in school who said you are ugly was angry because she was jealous of your looks, or she didn't get enough love in her own house and felt mean and angry. She wanted to hurt someone to feel better. Yes, that's right! People who feel bad because they don't get enough love deliberately hurt others to make them hurt more than they do themselves. They do feel better about themselves but only for a short time. What they say to hurt someone else in those moments is not true, and you don't need to hold on to that anymore. My love, your face is your beautiful face, and I love you, and your face is part of you, so I love your face too."

I hope this is all coming together for you now as you see how all the parts of you are interlinked and how you have to heal wounds at their source. Remember, you are not fat, you *have* fat, and the fat is there as a result of how you have been treating your body combined with your body's chemistry, so say "I'm sorry. Please forgive me. Thank you. I love you" to the body beneath the fat. Say it over and over again and release the pain and heartache so that you feel stronger and can make better choices. You don't need to love the fat but you *do* need to stop hating your body.

You graduate from this exercise when you can do it completely naked in front of a mirror. Getting to this point could take years; it took me years, but I did it. And I know you can too.

Sacred Intimacy with Your Body

The female body is designed to create—to grow and nurture babies, to grow and nurture anything we desire. We are born with all the eggs we need to have all the babies we are ever going to have. We go through transformation when we ripen in puberty to create breasts that will flood with rich, nutritious milk to feed a baby after it is born. Our womb ripens every month just in case an egg becomes fertilized, and we make a sacred space for the baby to grow every month. When that doesn't happen, we release the sacred blood. And when our bodies become too old to house a baby, these cycles slow down and stop, and our bodies become vessels with which we can create, grow, and nurture other things—anything really, as long as we embrace the flow of life force that runs within us, rather than deciding that life is over and battling against aging along with all the other things we tend to fight.

Being a woman is not a curse, nor is it something to get upset about. Life flows through our veins, our pores, and we run with it in natural cycles. Just as I said earlier, you don't have to love your fat, the body beneath the fat, or the menstrual blood, either. You don't need to do a moon dance, but if your body runs in a cycle that is affected by the moon, honor it if you feel called to. You don't need to do anything that feels wrong to you, but you do have to love your body for its miraculous ability to do whatever it was designed to do. If your body is infertile, there are gifts in that too.

We all write sacred contracts before we are born with other souls we will meet along the way. These contracts describe the lessons we will learn because we are here to grow. Contracts happen outside of our conscious mind, so we may not be aware of the lessons in advance. Our lesson may be to come to terms with a body that won't conceive, or it may be coming to terms with a body that conceives too easily. Aging and embracing our body in all of its cycles, stages, and beauty, are important lessons too.

Now that you feel safe to relax and have forgiven your body and all its parts, you will be feeling more comfortable in your skin. It's time to open your power, magic, creative aspect, sexuality—all of it. How does that sound to you? Walking in the world as a creative, sexual being can bring up a lot of fear, so let's clear it so the world becomes filled with beauty. Let's ensure the world is filled with people who don't cling to each other out of need and desperation—let the world be filled with people who are grounded, wholesome, and authentic. We want these people to support each other, grow healthy children with healthy attitudes, and in community bring Mother Earth back to a level of fertility so we can sustain each other as we were designed to do.

Tantric Body Connection

Tantra is a Hindu practice that means weaving and expanding energy. For me, tantra means being fully in the moment, slowing everything down, and becoming aware of all sensation, letting the sensations carry me instead of the mind. You've done great groundwork already for this if you've been doing the exercises up to this point. To be clear, I'm not offering you tantra doctrines, yoga, or mantras. If you want to go deeper with it, it's all there for you. What

I offer here is a way to go deeper with what you've been doing already.

The health of any relationship you have is based on the health of the relationship you have with yourself. So if you're unable to be intimate with yourself, then you can't really be intimate with someone else. All those hidden rooms you've locked inside yourself are showing themselves now, and you do not ever have to open them, truly. But if you want to, you will be able to find them with the work we are doing here. See this as a starting point; there's always more you can do.

Exercise
Tantric Body Connection

The agenda here is to slow down, connect to a source of love, and breathe that love into every part of your body. It's not about having an orgasm, but it is about opening parts of you, including your sexuality, to yourself, so you have a deeper connection with yourself. And you can allow yourself to have an orgasm if it surfaces; allow your body to wake up, light up, and shine its light. Pleasure of this kind is all natural; you were made this way. So let's celebrate our bodies instead of shutting them down.

> Be in your safe space for a set amount of time, say thirty minutes. Make sure you won't be disturbed and that you feel safe and contained. Slow down and breathe and come into your body, like we did in the "It is Safe to Relax" exercise. Don't be in a rush to do this part, as it is about a deeper connection to your body. Bring yourself right through your body, right down your legs and into the ground. Connect to Mother Earth and feel her

energy holding you. Allow your energy to expand so you can feel how much energy you can hold when you are feeling relaxed and at peace.

Just as in the healing work we did earlier in the book, imagine a pure source of unconditional love energy and ask to be connected to it. Let it flow into your physical body through the top of your head. Breathe it in and notice how warm it feels, how rich and tender it is as you use your breath to draw it down through the top of your head and into your face, neck, shoulders, arms, and chest. With every breath, it relaxes you even more. Breathe this unconditional love into your heart, stomach, hips, and root. Breathe it down your legs. Breathe out anything in you that is not love. You can recite the ho'oponopono too if you want and get lost in the energy of love, connecting the love to the different parts of your body, slowing down, and really bringing your attention to all of yourself. Visualize this loving energy, this pure source of forgiveness healing all of your wounds, releasing all of the deep hidden emotion that keeps you from your true authenticity. Let the emotions out if you need to. Go slowly, deliberately, and stay focused on love.

Now allow yourself to feel. Run your fingers along your skin. Simply the touch of your index finger on the inside of your wrist, if you like. Feel the sensation of skin on skin, of loving touch. Notice how different it feels when you are slow, when you are conscious and deliberate. You can feel the loving touch of your fingertips long after they have moved on to another part of your body. Keep

consciously connecting into that pure source of unconditional love, feel it flowing into your body through your
head, into your heart, over your shoulders, down your
arms, and into both of your hands. It's as if your hands
and fingertips are supercharged with a pure, loving
energy. Visit the places in your body you have hurt
the most with your criticism, and give them tender
love through your presence, through your fingertips.
Place your palms on your stretch marks and tell your
stomach that it's going to be okay, that you're here, that
you can connect to love, that there is nothing here but
love. Let your hands go where they will and stroke, glide,
touch, and heal your body. Let yourself feel the pleasure
of being touched by love, and let yourself feel the pleasure of touching with love. It can be overwhelming, so
go slowly and gently with yourself. Know that everything
you need is right here. Open up this part of yourself to
yourself, and you will never abandon yourself again.

Take time to close down from this exercise. Because
there is so much love being invoked, know that it takes
time to embody it and to ground yourself back into the
day. You might like to do this exercise before bedtime, so
all you have to do is cuddle up and have beautiful, loving
dreams. Or you might want to have a nap afterward, or
slowly dance and move your body into action again. You
could walk barefoot, feel fresh air on your face, or have
a cup of tea. Honor the time after the intimacy with a
transition to gently come back into reality rather than
rush back into your daily activities.

Being a Woman Is Magical

In the chapters to come we will look at our inner power and how to become the powerful beings we were meant to be. For now, know that spending time with your body and healing your Divine Feminine mother wound are so important. Notice how your life changes when you let more love and beauty in—you're the one removing the barriers between you and love. You may shift in your interests, find new friends, listen to new music, or wear different clothes. You might find yourself being nicer to yourself as your most natural state of being.

Healing the relationship you have with yourself enables healthy relationships between you and other women, other men, and between loving partners. Because you now know how to do it, you can heal yourself with love, allow yourself to open to love, and know that you are in control as the one who is offering the love to you. With the holding of Mother Earth, you can learn how to trust yourself more and make that commitment to your own health, which is how you heal your inner wounds. You are the one giving the permission to heal, you are the one doing the work, and you are the one who feels the benefits. In addition, we all feel the benefits from you doing your work too.

Affirmations for Connection to the Divine Feminine

If you're feeling shaky or hesitant about connecting to the beautiful, nurturing energies of the Divine Feminine, here are some affirmations that might help. They work well for both men and women, so see which ones work for you, for now. Change them up if you want to, and come back to this list if you outgrow them and need something else. Remember the 100 percent rule: you must believe the affirmation 100 percent for it to work.

- I am not my mother, I am myself.

- I am entitled to make my own choices.

- I can live my life the way that I want.

- I open my heart and forgive everything.

- I connect to the energies of the Divine Feminine and I am safe.

- Mother Earth can hold me today.

- I ask pure Divine Feminine energies to surround me and fill all my spaces with love.

Chapter 5

The Divine Masculine

This chapter is about getting in touch with the masculine energies and healing the wounding that stems from there, which could happen at any stage of your life.

I will not pretend to be a man, nor will I pretend to know what it feels like to have a man's body. However, we are all a combination of masculine and feminine energies, and I have worked with both energies with women and men.

A woman whose Divine Masculine energy is out of balance can be angry, forceful, and hard on the inside. Her emotions shut down and she focuses on action and achievement. A man whose Divine Masculine is out of balance is the same. We are all human and we need to learn how to support each other and to heal.

So no matter your gender, read the following chapter with an open mind, heart, and soul. Allow your Divine Feminine and Divine Masculine energies a chance to activate within you and have their say.

Here I work with the Divine Masculine, and though this chapter is written for all readers, I address it to the men. Having a strong Divine Masculine energy within me and having worked with many male clients, the content is very familiar to me. I urge all women to read this chapter just as I urge all male readers to read the previous chapter on the Divine Feminine so that we can understand the blending of the energies we are all composed of and learn how to balance them better.

We are all different: different cultures, different histories, different contracts and blueprints to our souls. There are different blends within each individual—the masculine woman, the feminine man; it's not that they are out of balance, it's just the way the masculine and feminine have mixed within. No matter what sex your body is, no matter whether you're more feminine than masculine or the other way round, the key to healing anything is stripping away the lies and standing in the truth. Being authentic inside and out.

Compared to the knowledge out there about the Divine Feminine, it seems as if there is little to no information available about the Divine Masculine energy. Women tend to talk and share to support each other; they write about how to do this and teach others to do the same. Women's circles span back centuries, and the wise woman or crone was always a figurehead in the community. Not so for men. Men's sheds are only becoming more common of late, and men are still figuring out what they need to be, and how to support other men and boys in their masculinity as they awaken. This in itself is part of the wounding of the Divine Masculine—the "shut up, buck up, shape up, and get on with it" attitude of the male stereotype. It creates an environment where men bottle up their feelings, stand up tall and strong, and do what they think they have to do without really knowing who they are and what they are capable of. I celebrate the men who gather in groups, share their emotions, celebrate each other's successes, and hold space for grieving.

I believe the Divine Masculine wound stems from a loss of identity, not knowing how to be a man, or what being a man actually means. In this world where women are fighting for equal standing and recognition, boys look to their fathers to set a standard of ideals in how to be a man in the world. However, there was nobody to tell their father what being a man means either, and there is no formal initiation into manhood in Western society. There are no guidelines, mentors, or instruction books around how to be a man. And in the meantime, women power ahead, activating their inner Divine Masculine, forging paths in places where before only men could tread. Women fight the good fight for empowerment, equality, and social justice...and men, well, they're not really sure if they're supposed to support the women or fight against them, and they're doing both. I think the biggest unnamed fear is this: "If women can hold down all the power jobs *and* have babies, why do men exist at all?" Some of my male clients have admitted as much to me.

Loss of purpose and identity leads to anger, resentment, depression, and addiction. It leads to broken relationships and self-sabotage. These are the things I work with in session and some of the things I want to work with in this chapter. And so you know where I'm coming from before we begin, I want you to know that I don't believe that men and women are equal; we are just not made the same. I also believe that every individual is different to every other individual, man *or* woman, and all of us are valuable. No matter our culture, skin color, gender, balance of masculine or feminine energies, I believe we are all fragments of Source energy, exploring and learning and growing in our own way. For this reason, I am passionate in my belief that every individual is as valuable as the next—and that includes you. Feeling like you are not of value or worthwhile is what I'm here to help heal in you. The feelings of powerlessness and being lost and alone are what I'm here to help you heal in yourself.

I'm not here to write a treatise on women versus men; I am here to help you heal your inner core wounding, no matter where it stems from. I am here to pull you up and out of feeling lost and alone and directionless. We'll recalibrate your inner navigation system so you feel more strong in your footing, more grounded in your outlook, more certain in who you are, and more clear about what you want. Once you feel oriented in life, have set goals and a direction, have a code of ethics installed in you and know who you are, it makes it easier to move forward, and moving forward is what Divine Masculine energy does best. Like an arrow shot forth from a bow, we are moving toward a target with power, motivation, and determination. That's the Divine Masculine in action.

What Does It Mean to You to Be a Man?

What does it mean to you to be a man? Stand tall, shoulders high, don't cry, don't feel, be strong, carry the load without complaining? Where did you get your ideas from? Do they stem from the values you had as a teenager or do you get them from heroes on television and in the movies? It's worth revisiting your values of what a man is supposed to be in your mind so you can better see where you fit into it and whether you've decided that you don't fit the bill at all. Think about the superhero, politician, priest, king, wizard, warrior, cowboy, soldier, sailor, and so on. Role models are ideals that encompass values that (hopefully) you've revisited with your inner teen. When looking at the ideal role model for the Divine Masculine, you can see that it encompasses quite a lot of strong values that may not be possible to carry off in reality.

A client came to me because he felt like he had failed at life; he had problems feeling close to his partner in romantic relationships. When he sensed the level of intimacy increase, he would distance himself or disappear and then hate himself for it. In session we discovered that he had a created an ideal man stereotype that became fixed in his mind when he was seven years old. He had never taken the time to realize that he had done this, so we did more work to understand firstly where this idea came from, and secondly why he always felt like he had failed. It turned out that his ideal man was a great adventurer, held the door open for women, paid for dinner, was an amazing dancer, made lots of money, was very sporty, could fix anything that was broken, never swore, and could always be depended on in an emergency. When I asked my client if his ideal man was based on his father, he replied, "No way! My father drank too much; I was afraid of him. He was always angry, came home late, was mean to my mom, and he never helped around the house." After doing further work he realized that he created this "perfect" man in his mind to counteract the behavior his father was displaying. He remembered hiding in his room one night hearing his father shout at his mother, making her cry. He swore to himself that he would never, ever be like him. That's the seed he planted in himself that somehow grew into this idea of the man that he thought he needed to be yet could never actually live up to. So as he failed to be this man, over time, he started to resent himself, which disempowered him and created low self-esteem. Even though my client was an amazing problem solver and a good listener with many other talents, he really didn't like himself at all. He discovered that the reason he didn't stay in relationships was because he didn't trust himself to behave well, just like his father hadn't. We deconstructed his idea of the perfect man, just as we are going to do here in the next exercise. My client realized that he didn't need to live up to any ideal—all he needed to be was the best version of himself at all times. That's really what personal growth and healing is all about.

I asked another client once what being a man meant to him. He said two words to me: "James Bond." So I asked him whether he thought treating women like objects, being shut off from his feelings, easily carrying out acts of violence, and keeping secrets and lying were the behaviors he aspired to. He didn't even realize that this is what James Bond was doing; he was just carried away by the romance and the fantasy of it all. Fantasy is fine and good and there is a place for it, but a real man is closer to the multidimensional man you are already than to a two-dimensional character in a movie. We will look more at shadow and light in chapters 6 and 7, but for now it's important that you can disconnect your ideal man from a fantasy man who doesn't exist. This also goes for feminine roles too, such as the perfect mother, career woman, and so on. Stereotypes eat into both our subconscious and our conscious mind and influence us more than we know. Are you constantly thinking in stereotypes?

Stripping Down to the Truth

Just as I had you revisit your values when you were doing the work of the inner teen, it's time to look at your values when it comes to what it means to be a man ... or a woman too! If you didn't do the work of the inner teen, it might be relevant here, so take a look at that exercise in chapter 2 first, and then come back and try this one next. Just like my clients, you could be quite surprised at what you are subconsciously trying to live up to.

Exercise

Journaling

Get a notebook and write down your thoughts about each of the bullet points that follow. You can write as much as you need. Think about your life and how your thoughts might have influenced your actions and your feelings about yourself in the past. Don't wallow in regret; this is an observational exercise to get to know yourself and how you are thinking. Know by doing this exercise, you're doing work to heal yourself, and that's the most important thing you can do for yourself.

- What does being a man mean to you?

- Describe your ideal man. Do you feel that you are living up to that role model? Why?

- Is there any part of "being a man" that you enjoy? What is it?

- Is there any part of "being a man" that you don't enjoy? Why?

- Where did you get your ideas about what a man should be? Are they true?

- If you could change anything about your ideas now, what would that be?
- How does being a man affect you when it comes to:
  - Body shape/size/stature/strength
  - Expressing emotion/sensitivity
  - Providing for a family/getting the job done
  - Having fun/playfulness
- Name a man in real life that you admire. List the qualities that he has. Are these qualities you have, or qualities that you aspire to have? Why?

Know that it might be your inner child who answers some of these questions, so take a break, go for a walk, or come back another day to do this next part. You need to call on your responsible adult self when you look back at your answers so that you'll notice if and where you drift off into childish thinking. Knowing what you do now as the adult, what do you have to say to yourself about what you wrote? If you need to, you can educate your inner wounded child.

Educate Your Inner Wounded Child

Before you do this exercise you need to be clear with yourself that it is safe to feel your emotions, that you are allowed to cry as a way to release big emotions, and that love is something that you can allow into your heart. If you need to do more work on opening yourself up to compassion and love, please revisit chapter 1, and bring with you your ideas on what your role model looks like versus who your father was versus the reality that there are warm, loving husbands and fathers out there. Even if you didn't have one, you have the potential to be one. You truly do, if you do your inner work. You might want to do the work of chapter 1 with a therapist for help going to difficult places emotionally. It helps quite a bit to receive confirmation and validation that you are healing the wound of the abandoned inner child, and the knowledge that you are able to open your heart to love.

Exercise

Connect to Your Inner Child

Take some space and time for yourself to do some inner work.

Close your eyes, breathe, and slow down; bring your awareness into your body.

If you're feeling jittery, angry, or emotional because of what you need to say, remember that you are the adult here so you need to be grounded.

Breathe your awareness all the way down your body, down your legs, and into the floor. Feel your grounding cords going from your feet deep into the ground beneath you. Breathe in the nourishing nurturing energies of Mother Earth. She's always here for you, and it doesn't make you any less of a man to work with her.

When you feel more balanced and stable, when your breath is slow and you feel safe, visualize a space in nature.

Invite your inner child, the age that you were when you created these fixed ideas, to come meet you and talk with you.

Connect to a source of love inside of you so that when you see yourself as a child, you feel compassion for what you were going through at the time.

Gently talk to your wounded child. Ask questions and listen, and then point out where some of the thinking is now out of date, where you have learned new things and can see and feel the value of yourself as an individual in the world. Don't railroad your inner child—they want to learn, and by your example you're showing them what a real man is like, instead of the idea of the ideal man that they created.

If you need to make a commitment to learn something new, take better care of yourself, or visit somewhere or someone, then do that.

Open your heart to your inner child: allow a light in your heart to shine brightly...and see their inner light shine in response. Feel love flowing between you both; smile and hug each other if you're able to.

Tell your inner child you will meet them again. Give them some time to process what you've discussed.

Let the images dissolve away and bring yourself back into the room. Feel how you are feeling. Take some time to embody the work before going back into busy daily activities.

You can share your thoughts about what being a man means with a friend, and it might inspire you to hear what another man has to say about this very same thing. Men need to talk with other men about what being a man means, and if you found the exercise above profound, perhaps your friend will benefit too. It's always good to stop and think about our fixed ideas, as they limit and restrict us, particularly when some of the pain you may be feeling could be coming from not being able to live up to a fixed ideal that you created as a child.

Smash the Ideal Man and Be Who You Are

So you need to let go of the idea of who you think you should be, and allow yourself to be who you actually are. Removing masks from your personality, the exercise from chapter 2 is very worthwhile; I recommend doing it if you've not done it, particularly as it relates to this work. And you need to stop asking, "What would a real man/ideal man do in this situation?" You need to believe in yourself that you are, in fact, a real man. You heard me right— you are a real man. So it's time to own that, particularly as you've learned at this point that your idea of a "real man" isn't real at all. If you ground to the earth (energetically), just as we did in chapter 4, you will feel held, and once you feel held, you can shed the skin that you have grown out of, the skin of pretense. It's really about being who you are, not being what you think you should be. When I say "smash the ideals" I'm saying smash your idea of who you think you need to be, and become comfortable with who you *are* in your entirety. You don't fit a mold—you create the mold for you.

If you want to go deeper with this, have a look at my book *How to Be Well,* where I bring you through a process of reidentification, starting with the aspects of you (mind, body, emotions, spirit), the labels that you placed on yourself (or were placed upon you), and the relationships you define yourself by, to shed all of it and discover the vibrant soul beneath the complex and flawed personality.

It also includes some work to improve that personality too! All personalities have flaws, even mine—that's what makes us human. We strive to be the best we can be, flaws and all.

Healing is not a cure for living, it's a process, a flow—healing happens when we are in motion. We all have good days and bad days. Allowing yourself to be completely yourself is the biggest gift you can ever give yourself; it's the freedom to stretch your wings, take the leap, and be the talented, gifted person you have the potential to be.

Merging the Ideal with the Real

There's an Irish joke where someone asks directions to somewhere far away, and the person giving the directions says, "Ah, well you can't get there from here; you have to go back down into the town and start from there!"

The truth is, wherever you have been, and wherever you are going, you have to meet yourself where you are right now and make your next move from here. What's important to realize about your ideal self, is that as you grow and change, your idea of what is ideal for you also grows and changes. So if you are moving forward on a timeline, as you move forward, your ideal self also moves forward. So you will actually never catch up with him. And because he doesn't actually exist, it's time to release the pressure you put on yourself to be him. It can be hard to process this idea, so if you need to, take some time out now, and make sure you understand that you, just as you are, are enough. Working on you, on improving yourself, transforming things in you, is all you need to do. You don't need to be anybody else. Just being you is enough.

Let's look at the gap between the ideal self in your mind that you are trying to live up to (who is, by the way, becoming more and more like you the more you think about this), and who you actually are. There are a few ways you can do this. I'll share one way for your logical mind, and an energetic healing practice that you can do for your spirit, and you might come up with a few other ways to do it for yourself once you get started.

Working with the Mind

After talking to your wounded child, your existing thought patterns may need to change. Working with the mind is always a separate exercise from working with the emotions, and wounded child work is emotional. You have to approach logical thinking work in a different way. You could be punishing yourself unknowingly by criticizing yourself constantly because your ideal self would have achieved so many things at your age already that you may not have. You need to do two things here: look at what it is that you think you want to be doing and start doing it (external work), *and* you need to be nicer to yourself in your self-talk (internal work). Both of these things are difficult, but possible.

Exercise

Unraveling Your Thoughts

- What is it you think your ideal self should be doing/ would have already done that you cannot live up to?

- Are you harboring a grudge against yourself because of this? How does that express itself through the language of your self-talk?

- Is this something that you're truly interested in doing? If yes, how can you do it in a realistic way? If no, how can you truly let it go so you're no longer holding yourself to it?

Whatever you come up with can be a big thing like being married, having children, or traveling the world, or a small thing like being sporty. That said, being sporty can be a big thing depending on the scope of your ambition. If you're wanting to be a champion tennis player, for example, and are in your sixties and have never played tennis before, you're not going to make the Wimbledon Championships anytime soon. So allow yourself to move on from it, and take the time to give yourself the tools and support you need while you make the changes you need to make. I know many men who were doing a similar thing subconsciously, and stuck with the tennis once they realized they didn't have to be a champion; they simply wanted to play. They got great pleasure out of playing tennis in their local club, and winning a few matches there the odd time. It fulfilled that need in them.

Do you see where I'm coming from? You don't have to be the football star, but you might want to play football three nights a week down at the local club. You don't need to run for parliament, but perhaps you'd like to try public speaking at the local toastmasters, or run for a position on a committee. It takes the pressure off, doesn't it?

There are lots of things you can do to actively be out in the world doing things rather than looking at someone else doing the extreme version of that thing and deciding you'll never be good enough to be as skilled as them. You have to start somewhere, and projecting a need or a desire onto an ideal without taking action to cultivate that need or desire in yourself disempowers you and creates resentment and low self-esteem, leading to low self-worth. Remember, even the experts were beginners once.

Working with fixed thought patterns is a difficult task, and you might need to get some help. You can keep it logical and do work with Cognitive Behavioral Therapy (CBT), which helps transform unhealthy thought patterns, or you could look at Neurolinguistic Programming (NLP), which does a similar thing. You could also look into the Emotional Freedom Technique (EFT) to break the energy behind your thought patterns. Learning where you are now, however, is where you must begin.

Exercise

Learn What You're Doing to Yourself

Write down the language you use when you're criticizing yourself. Feel into the tone of the words, and really immerse yourself in the vibration of the sentence so you recognize it when you're doing it subconsciously. Now write down an antidote to this criticism in a gentle but firm tone, something like "Yes, that's what my father wanted me to do, but I'm not actually interested in doing that. I'm living my life for me, not for him." You can then use this antidote anytime you catch your inner critic tearing you down.

The most important thing is to learn what your patterns are so you can change them. Catching yourself talking down to yourself in a mean and nasty way can be a shock the first few times you do it because there's a part of you that is able to tune it out. However, you're not immune to it—each time you do it it's as if you're putting poison into your system. When you hear yourself saying things to yourself that are hurtful or that you'd never dream of saying to anyone else, use your antidote. Without judgment—seriously, if you start to criticize yourself for having those thoughts, you're actually creating another pattern you will eventually need to break—catch the thought and address it directly, like it's a person separate from you. You can say, "Hold on a moment now. What exactly was that you just said?" and transcribe it in a notebook as if you're in court and want the exact phrase. Collect these exact phrases (you don't need to show them to anyone) as you might collect rocks. You can take a time-out after you've collected quite a few of them to categorize them. Look at the words you use, put similar ones together, and see what the general gist is, like organizing your rock collection. However, what you've arranged are not rocks—they're poisons. Different poisons with different strengths and potencies. So take some time to work with each poison and create an antidote—words as medicine to heal, instead of poison to harm. I'll give you a few examples:

Poison: I'm a fool, a complete idiot, how could I have done that thing again?

Antidote: I didn't see that coming. I missed a chance but it will come around again. Everything will be okay, just give it some time. If it is meant to be, then it will be.

Poison: It's all my fault everything is so shitty in my life. I'm totally useless; I'll never be good enough.

Antidote: As hard as it is, I do realize now that I did the best I could with what I had and knew at the time. I will learn how to forgive myself and move on so that I can create a life I love.

There are lots of affirmations around that can act as antidotes to your poisonous thoughts. It's worth putting the time in to really make sure that the antidotes work. And how do you know if they work? See how you feel when you read the poisonous statements above out loud, and follow them by reading the antidote.

What happens next is recognizing the toxic thought as it's coming out of your head, or even before it's formed. Then you have your antidote ready, you think it (some clients say it out loud for the extra power), and it neutralizes the toxin. Doing this gives you a break. It's a dance: responsible adult versus saboteur (the very angry part of you). Once you keep up with the antidote, the angry part of you usually subsides or tries another way to hurt you. I'm not leaving you high and dry; I say it as it is. We will look at anger management in the next part of this chapter, and in chapter 6 I will cover shadow work, where you can work directly with the saboteur aspect of you.

Meet Who You Are Becoming

Somewhere in the future is a healed version of you, so proud of all the work you are doing now so you can become him. Connect to the self you are now, and accept who you are; then you can feel into the trajectory of where you're going and who you are becoming. The following exercise uses visualizations, but if you're not good at visualizing with your eyes closed, you might like to draw this as a piece of artwork instead. Or do both! Sometimes putting energy work into form, i.e., drawing on a page, makes the visualization more powerful and real for your mind. Similar to making the masks, the kinesthetic work of feeling and touching that healed self makes it real and can make more of an impression on you and reinforce the healing work.

Exercise

Meeting Your Future Healed Self

Visualize yourself with a white background, in this present moment now, as you are, flaws and all, wearing what you are wearing. Say hello to yourself!

Visualize your ideal man. Notice how far away he is from you, and in which direction. What is he wearing? How is he holding himself? What may he be thinking of you?

Place the two of you in your mind so it feels like you are here, and he is somewhere in your future timeline. Ask yourself how long it will take for you to grow into him. The answer you receive will define the distance between you both.

Imagine now that you are leaving yourself here and traveling up along the timeline to meet him. Notice as you're doing this that he looks softer and more like you and less like a stranger you couldn't ever become. Because you've placed him on your timeline, in your future, there is a possibility that you can become him. Just be with how that feels for a while, and notice what is going on emotionally for you … and for him too! I can imagine him smiling at you, proud of you, happy to see you, with wisdom to give to you about how you can move from where you are in life to where he is.

Feel free to ask him any question about anything, and make the space for him to answer. What does he say? How is the relationship between you both? How do you feel when you talk to him?

Say goodbye to him and shake his hand or even hug him if you feel it's appropriate. Leave him where he is, and bring yourself back to yourself in the present moment. How does that feel? What has changed?

As your ideal man becomes more like you in the future, feel a shift in your heart around how you are feeling about yourself. Perhaps you want to move him down the timeline so he is closer to you now than he was. Don't do this logically, let it just shift and change by itself.

Now that you can see him closer to you, he is less of an ideal and more like your future healed self. He is you in the future, when you are healed from this wounding. How does that sit with you?

Now mark on the timeline the point between where you are now and where he is. Go there and step out of the timeline into a park with a park bench. Sit on the bench and wait, and he will join you there. If you want to continue your conversation with him from here, go ahead.

Make sure when you've finished your chat that you come back in your mind's eye to this present moment in time, that the timeline and your future healed self have dissolved from your awareness. Bring yourself completely back to the now moment. Well done!

Go to the park bench in your mind's eye anytime you want to, and meet your future healed self. Know that he is you in the future: over this issue, successful and happy in his life, and doing the things he loves. Make it feel as real as you can, because only that way will it truly come to pass. And the real beauty of this exercise is that each time you visit, the space on the time-line between the present moment and where your future healed self resides shortens because you're doing your work. Remember also that it doesn't shorten incrementally or logically either, it can shorten in fits and bumps, in jumps and leaps, depending on your breakthroughs, and how dedicated you are to the task.

Being You Is Enough

How do you feel now? Are you feeling happier to be you? Does knowing that you can make these improvements in yourself, by yourself, and that they are possible take pressure off you? Make a commitment to do work on yourself every day, to be kind and gentle to yourself, to use your antidotes and learn how to stop poisoning yourself, and to visit your future healed self and ask him for help.

Managing Anger

Some men believe that being angry is part of being a man. They wear their anger as a badge of honor and make no excuses for their behavior. This mindset is not acceptable—anger of any kind can make the angry person sick as well as hurt the people around them. I see anger as an indicator something is wrong, and if whatever's wrong is not fixed or changed, the anger eventually turns inward and becomes destructive, depressive, and damaging.

Anger as an emotion doesn't care where it comes from or what caused it; it builds up onto itself over time until a low level simmering anger becomes a pressure cooker of anger, and it only takes one small thing to set off an explosion. So there are two parts to managing anger: what you do in the moment when you're expressing from a place of anger, and how to deal with that pressure cooker of anger within, when you're in a more grounded state of mind.

If you're still reading this, I'm proud of you. Truly—I'm not being funny here. Keep an open mind and try these exercises, even if you're not sure whether you're angry or not. We are all experts at hiding things from ourselves and have been taught that anger is not an appropriate response, hence our tendency to hide that too.

Releasing the Wellspring of Anger

Most people are not aware of their anger when they are not angry because they have become experts at hiding it from themselves. Many female clients say that their partners are furiously angry most of the time and deny it or are genuinely not aware of it, so it makes it very difficult to move through it without setting them off.

Anger is a heavy and slow energy, a weight that really slows you down, consumes your energy, and causes stagnation, which is the opposite of what Divine Masculine energy is all about. Allow yourself to discover what is going on subconsciously for you and let yourself release the emotions, feeling your feet on the ground and letting them move through you, breathing through it just like we did in "The Safe Release of Grief" in chapter 3. You might like to revisit that exercise before you go deep into this one.

Exercise

Release the Wellspring of Anger

Create a space where you feel safe, grounded, calm, and relaxed. Set your purpose and intention to discover how much anger you're carrying inside you today (it can change from day to day). You can work with the image of a well if you want, or you can picture containers or vats of toxic liquid, or let your subconscious show you what your anger feels like to you in a dreamlike landscape.

When you're ready, imagine a cinema screen behind your eyes; the projector is your subconscious mind. Ask yourself to show yourself how much unprocessed anger you're carrying around with you. It can come as quite a shock to see how much anger you're carrying, so stay grounded and just be with the image. You can handle it without judgment as you come into balance with it. It might be enough for one sitting to just get used to the idea that you're carrying around a lot of anger, and it can take a while to process.

While you're still with the image, you can categorize the anger, if you want, into old anger, new anger, childhood anger, other people's anger, anger around feeling power-less, anger at yourself. I see men moving vats into different piles and labeling them so that they have a workflow organized. The labeling is not very important, but it might give you an idea of where your work lies, and it can be healing to realize that even though it seems overwhelming, not all anger comes from the same source. It might also make you feel sad to realize just how much you're carrying. If you can, forgive yourself for not realizing what you were doing. Knowing what you now know, you can make the commitment to not let it get this bad again, but don't blame yourself for letting things get this bad, as you did the best you could with what you knew.

Now you're going to transmute (i.e., sublimate, dissolve away, or transform into something healing rather than toxic) some of this anger. This is energetic work, so you don't need to do anything in the real world. Use your imagination and give yourself permission to let it go, take time with it, sit with it, let the energies do the work. Here are a few things you can do:

- Ask that all the anger you've inherited be dissolved away because it is not your job to carry it anymore. If nothing shifts, make sure that all of the aspects of you (including your inner helpful teenager) are in alignment with your healing this anger. If they are misaligned, make a note of it and do some work with them to reassure them that you in fact don't have to carry your grandfather's frustrations anymore.

- Use your breath to breathe out the anger from the stockpile, and tune in to a source of peace and breathe it in to soften and transform your images. As you breathe in, let go of tension, rage, and anger. As you breathe out, you can imagine the image that illustrates your anger softening, melting, changing color to something paler, dissolving, draining, or disappearing slowly, in its own time. Please don't force this, because if you do, you step out of the energy work and into the mind. Being forceful with it isn't healing it, it's just putting desire into an active fantasy. The anger will still be there in your subconscious, but you can convince yourself it's gone if you want to ... though it kind of defeats the purpose.

- Get some energetic help. Ask the angels or your future healed self to show you what to do, or call on a power animal to help you with this. The power animal I love to use in situations like this is a dragon who breathes fire on the stockpile and transforms it that way. Burying it as it is won't help because you're just pushing it deeper into your subconscious. You want to clear it, not hide it. The angels can light a bonfire; you and your future healed self can pile your anger onto it and watch it burn away. Again, it can help if you tune in to a source of peace and inhale peace, exhale the anger.

When you've spent ten or twenty minutes with this exercise, stop. As I said before, you can't force this work. Your body will be tired from doing it. You might need to take a rest, and you will need to take time to come into balance with the changes to notice how you feel on the inside and what is different about your behavior. Come back to do this exercise a few times, maybe once every few days to start, then once a week, then once every couple of weeks, depending on how much of a problem anger is for you or for your partner. Notice if the stockpile builds up again between sessions or if it stays the same ... or if it dissolves away by itself over time. Don't be disheartened if it does build up. Keep going with your work, and don't forget that you can check in with your inner child and inner teen to make sure they're not going out looking for additional sources of anger behind your back.

In the Moment of Anger

It's so hard to manage anger when you're angry, but if you're successful at drawing down the wellspring so your levels are not full to brimming, you will be more likely to catch yourself in the act. When you do catch yourself, the simplest and easiest thing to do is stop. Stop! That's all. Simply catch yourself midsentence. Stop, and breathe. Feel your feet on the ground and remember who you are, and that it's not worth lashing out. Breathe out the anger, send it into the earth, and gather your thoughts. Bring yourself back into the present moment. If you're able to take it one step further, notice if your energy field has shrunk or contracted, and as you breathe, slow down even more and visualize your energy field expanding outward again. When we feel threatened, we shrink, get angry, and lash out. A small energy field leads to a low tolerance for anger, so you need to up your tolerance right away so you can engage with what is going on in front of you rather than obliterate it.

Once you've contained yourself, you can then decide if you need to take a time out, i.e., walk away and deal with the issue after you've had some time to think. If this is a relationship issue, and most things that cause explosive angry outbursts are, then it's much better to wait until the wave of anger has passed and your tolerance levels have improved. No matter how insistent your partner may be that they need to deal with this "right now," there are two of you in the relationship, and you have every right to say "not now, later" and commit to arranging a time later when you will be prepared to talk about the issue, in a calmer space. You don't have to arrange that particular time while you're angry, either; you can make an arrangement to talk about making an arrangement to talk. Seriously, if you give yourself and your partner lots of space to learn how to talk about relationship issues, you have lots of space for tolerance and compassion for each other too.

One more thing about managing live anger: don't berate yourself if you didn't catch it in the moment. Just like critical and nasty thoughts, you have to learn when and how you get angry before you can really change it. It does help to get some help with this, so if you know you have a tendency to be angry, make a time for that conversation with your partner in which you suggest they have a code word indicating they sense you're about to have an outburst of anger or are actually having one. Promise them that you'll take their word for it and stop, slow down, breathe, and ground yourself before continuing on, and they have to promise that they'll not use this code word for fun or to mess with you. If you're both serious about learning how to work through difficult issues, you have to both be the responsible adults that you are. You will be surprised at how well it works when you work together.

When You're Not Actively Angry But Things Still Make You Angry

You can't expect the triggers for your anger to disappear over time if you don't sort them out. A great time for you to work on this is actually when you're feeling good about yourself and the world, so list the things that make you angry or trigger your explosive, angry behavior, and make a plan for what you want to do about them. My assumption is that you don't want to carry anger and be easily triggered—go meet with your future healed self and ask him if he wants you to sort this out, or if he is still explosively angry and wants to remain so ... I didn't think so!

Sometimes I find that what makes us angry is less about the thing itself and more about how we feel about the thing. For example, a client who thought she hated her job actually didn't hate the actual job she had to do, she just didn't like the gossip and the relationships that were made between the people at work. She got muddled in her head about what her job was versus what her work environment was like and labeled the whole thing "job." Once she figured it out, she could disengage with gossip, change her desk, and stop interacting with certain people. She was much happier afterward. It's worth your taking the time to split out all of the different aspects of what it is you're angry about so you can nail down exactly what it is without taking it personally. Remember that everyone has a flawed personality. If someone else's behavior is angering you, it is possible that they're acting that way with other people as well as you. Talk about the issue with other people and do your research before deciding to never talk to that person again. If you are able to have a cool head while coming up with a solution, the situation will improve, even if it's not exactly the answer you were looking for.

It Is Safe to Feel

Truly knowing that it is safe to experience your emotions is so empowering. You take the power away from the fear that these emotions will break your life apart and can then use it for other, more useful things in your life. Men who do brave things still feel fear and anxiety about doing those things; it's what makes us human. Ask any man who has been to war if he was never anxious or scared, and you already know what they'll say. Anxiety, fear, guilt, shame, jealousy, and grief are all natural emotions we are designed to experience, which is the key—we are designed to experience them, not to lock them away and hope they disappear. They won't.

When it comes to organizing emotions, the way of the Divine Masculine psyche is to compartmentalize, or "put it into a box and put it away." Does this resonate? Over time, many of these compartments become filled with emotions that are saved up for later, except there is no "later"—there's only this moment, right now. Are you ready to discover how many of these containers you're carrying?

In this next exercise you're going to do an inventory of the containers of emotion you are carrying. If you're feeling worried about this already, be with the worry, connect into your inner wisdom and strength, and ask yourself if you're ready to do this discovery exercise. If not, ask what you need to do to get ready. Then do it. Then come back and try again. I didn't say it was going to be easy.

Exercise

Discovery

Make a quiet safe space for yourself where you won't be disturbed. Know that you're not going to open any of your boxes just yet; you're just going to get an idea of how many boxes you're carrying.

Breathe and relax and know that you are safe. Connect into the adult you are and talk to your inner child, if it's the child part of you who is upset or worried. They didn't do a bad thing by boxing up your emotions for you— they did what they felt they needed to do at the time. So reassure them that you're not mad at them, but it's time to clean up now and you just want to see how much work you have to do.

Visualize a space in your mind's eye where you feel safe. You are able to see the number of containers filled with emotion you are carrying. The space could be a warehouse, an art gallery, an open space in nature, or even your childhood school's auditorium.

Your containers don't have to be boxes, either; they could be treasure chests, ceramic pots, suitcases, or shopping bags. They are all different shapes and sizes. Allow the space you've chosen to show you how many of these containers you are carrying.

Breathe and relax and come into balance with what you're seeing in your mind's eye. As you breathe, relax your body and know that whatever it is … is what it is, and it's okay.

Once you've slowed your breathing and are more in balance with what you see in your mind's eye, ask yourself if this is all the boxes or if there are more. Allow more to appear.

Now breathe again, and come into balance again.

Imagine you're connecting to a source of healing energy, just like we have done before. Breathe the source of healing into your body, and feel it soften your body even more. Allow the tension in your body to melt and the hard parts of you to soften, and let yourself feel the flow of healing energy through your body.

Visualize your heart center shining like great golden sunshine radiating out from your chest, both in front of and behind you. Remember how much love you have access to for yourself and others.

Now look again at the containers. Ask that the ones which are no longer valid or serve you disappear.

With the light of love from your heart radiating outward, see some of the containers melting away until you are left with the ones that still have lessons for you, that still have gifts to reveal.

Breathe and come into balance again.

Now ask the containers to reorganize themselves—perhaps three or four of them could melt into one bigger one; perhaps the material the containers are made from could change so that a few suitcases melt into one bigger treasure chest. Let your subconscious mind do the work; just step back and watch, and stay connected to your inner light.

Once you feel the healing has occurred, you can say thank you to your higher self and the parts of you who showed up for this work. Allow the images to dissolve away and come back into the moment, into your body, and into the room.

I love how many of my clients do end up with treasure chests at the end of this exercise, or the idea of there being far fewer containers with precious information than they had thought. We put so much pressure on ourselves to do things the way we think they should be done and create most of these containers ourselves in this way. These containers only serve to show us that we don't need to do this, not anymore.

Opening and Healing the Containers of Emotion

I think you're able to guess what happens in this next piece of work. Knowing what you now know about how the subconscious works, you have awareness that the next time you visit the space where your healed containers are, they may look different again. Depending on the space of time between the above exercise and this one, you may also have created more of them. But after the experience of discovery, you only have to open one container at a time, discover the gift it has in there for you, and let it shrink or dissolve away.

All I'll say about this next piece of work is don't hold the image in your mind as the reality of the situation. It's only the reality of the moment, and the moment changes depending on what you're connecting to. I'd also suggest giving yourself plenty of time afterward if difficult emotions do come up so you can process them, write about them, or phone a friend.

Exercise

It Is Safe to Feel

Make a quiet safe space for yourself where you won't be disturbed. Breathe and bring your awareness into your body, slowing right down. Become aware of your heartbeat, your breathing, and any tension or pain in your physical body. The longer you spend doing this, the deeper and easier the healing will become. If the healing becomes too intense, come back to this, the pure sensation of simply being present in your body.

In your mind's eye, visualize the space where your containers of emotion reside. Perhaps it looks different ... more organized, tidier. Perhaps there are more containers than you expected, perhaps less. Take some time to see yourself wandering around among them, feeling and touching them, getting ideas of what they may be about. Remember, this is an abstract exercise so you may not have a logical explanation for what you are feeling, and that's okay. Don't let your mind and thoughts take you out of the healing process. You can journal later on if you want to analyze it, just like you wouldn't analyze a dream while you're in it.

See yourself sit down either beside a container you want to work with or in a space away from all of the containers. Connect to that healing light just as before, and breathe and let it into your body. Open your heart and feel the light shining out in front of you and behind you. Move on to the next step only when you feel ready.

Call upon one of the containers that's ready for you to work with. It can appear beside you or move toward you. If it seems reluctant to work with you, say thank you and maybe next time. Choose one that's actually ready.

You can open the container and look inside, see what's there. Shine your light of love and compassion upon it, knowing you did the best you could at that time with what you knew. Allow the emotion to surface.

With your awareness and compassion, the container starts to shrink and dissolve. You can place it on your lap and allow yourself to absorb the energy, letting the emotions move through you and out from you.

If you know what memory is attached to your repressed emotion, allow yourself to go back there and feel what you didn't want to feel at the time. Be the adult you are now, standing beside the person you were then, just like you've done for your inner child, teen, and young adult. Ask for the learning and wisdom to be retained, and let the emotions release. Then let go of the images, and feel what your body is feeling. Feel what your heart is experiencing. Be in whatever emotion you are in, and if you're not in one, know that the healing is working in the background and the work you've done to bring you to this point is what is standing with you now.

When you're ready, look down at your lap and see if there's a gift there for you from that memory or experience. It may be something obvious like a golden chalice for strength or a medal for bravery, or it might be something obscure, like a geometrical shape. Either way, that gift is active, vibrant, and means something to you or will over time. While still in the visualization, if you'd like, you can stand up and bring your gift to a cabinet where you can give it a space of honor. Or you can allow this gift to dissolve into your energy field if the learning has been received.

Breathe and come into balance with the work you have done. Slowly allow yourself to bring your awareness into the room you're in. Become aware of the sensation of your physical body and this moment in space and time. Let yourself come back to the room you are in. Take as long as you need to process this exercise.

This is a very powerful exercise, and is designed to be repeated. Don't open more than two boxes in one sitting or you won't properly process whatever is inside. Allow yourself to feel the lightness you feel afterward, knowing that the burden you carry is lessened. Some of my clients actually feel heavier after doing this work not because they've unearthed more work to do, but because the emotions were actually keeping them out of their body. In releasing, accepting, and not being afraid of those emotions, something inside of these clients softened and allowed them to come back into their bodies again. The heaviness is in fact the sensation of being in the body, *really* being there. It's beautiful.

Releasing Stagnation

Let's end this chapter with a free flow of energy to power up the Divine Masculine energies that are directive, powerful, and focused, creating positive action. Remember that although I've been looking at the many aspects of the Divine Masculine that go out of balance to help you heal them, there are also many wonderful aspects that when harnessed consciously, can really help you move through the sludge of life and get the work done.

When stagnant, masculine energies cause frustration, anger, and depression. You always have to do the work; just knowing what to do isn't enough.

So how do you release stagnant energies?

Moving the body around can really help. Going for a run, playing a game of football with friends, or even a gentle walk can get things moving on the physical level. If the stagnation is energetic, however, an energetic solution is required. Yoga, tai chi, or chi gong can help open up the energy centers in the body to release blockages and get your proverbial engine going again.

More and more, I am realizing that what we put into the body deeply influences what we get out of it. So look at your diet (garbage in, garbage out) and power up your food sources with fresh, healthy vegetables, fruit, and grains, and add in warming spices. Let go of processed, sugar-filled foods, and cut down on salt as well, because these heavy foods are very difficult for your body to metabolize. A heavy body leads to heavy attitude and heavy energies.

Power Up Your Energy

This exercise will help you release blocked energies in your body. Do it a few times over a short period of time, and you will notice a change in your overall attitude and energy levels. You are going to imagine the energy centers in your body activating, lighting up, and shining brightly, starting from the bottom and working their way up to the top. The energy center, when it's at its best, is a spinning wheel that moves clockwise in front of your body. See figure 1 to help you. There are seven main energy centers in the body, so before starting, decide how long you want to spend with each one of them, plus add in about five minutes on top of that for opening and closing space to help you decide how long you need for the work. You can set an alarm or a timer to help you keep track of where you are and what you need to do.

The image below is a guideline as to where the centers are and what they look like.

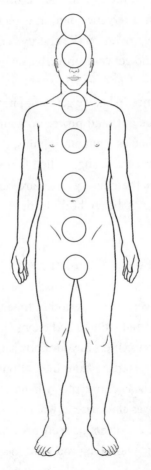

Figure 1: The body's energy centers.

Exercise

Powering Up Your Energy

Make a space where you won't be disturbed. Sit comfortably, wear comfortable clothing, and take your shoes off if you want to.

Start with the energy center that lies between your legs, usually visualized as a red spinning light. Use your imagination to get a picture of how it looks right now, then use your intention to ignite it. See it activating and lighting up. With every breath you focus on it, it gets stronger. Imagine the red light spinning and growing and becoming healthier as it spins. Spin it counterclockwise to empty out all the crud and dark, heavy energy you've been storing there, like an exhaust pipe. Then spin it clockwise again so it settles and comes into balance as a much brighter light than before. Notice how your body feels as you do this. Shift your position so you are more comfortable if need be. Stay here for as many minutes as you had decided in advance.

Move your awareness up to just below your stomach and let yourself tune in to the energy center here. Visualize an orange spinning light in your energy field coming out from just below your belly button. Before you begin, notice what sort of condition it is in. Do the same thing here as before: see it getting just as bright as the red one, spinning clockwise and bright, healthy and awake and alive. Then focus your awareness on the orange spinning light that shines out from behind you. Both centers shine front and back, and it's just as important to do the work there too. Again, stay here for as long as needed until you're happy that you have a healthy energy center, front and back.

Move your awareness now to the next center, just above your belly button. Let yourself see the yellow spinning light, front and back, just as it is. Then you can work on it with your breath and imagination, spinning it counter-clockwise and emptying it out, and then clockwise again. See the yellow spinning wheels becoming as bright as the red and orange lights, healthy and awake, active and alive. Stay here for as long as you want to.

Next, move your awareness up to your breastbone and imagine a green spinning light, front and back. Allow yourself to see it and then start your work. See it getting just as bright as the others as you finish; it should look like it's spinning clockwise and bright, healthy and awake and alive.

When you're ready, move your awareness up to your throat and imagine a blue spinning light, front and back. Do the clearing work and see it becoming as bright as the others, spinning clockwise and bright, healthy and awake and alive.

Move your awareness up to your forehead now and imagine an indigo spinning light, front and back. Open up the energy center and clear it, then see it becoming just as bright as the others, spinning clockwise and bright, healthy and awake and alive.

The last energy center that we are working with is at the top of your head. Move your awareness there and imagine a violet spinning light. This is the partner to the red light at the bottom, so take some time to clear it; see it getting just as bright as the others, spinning clockwise and bright, healthy and awake and alive.

If you want to, once you have cleared and activated all the seven centers, you can go visit them all again, one at a time to make sure that they're all healthy, in balance, and equal to each other. Notice if one is spinning faster or brighter than another or if one of them is still blocked. If so, don't worry. Just bringing your awareness to this work will really help.

Finally, sit and breathe. Relax and tune in to your lights and your body. Give yourself permission to feel, see, or know if you have any other blocks in your energy field. As you relax and breathe more deeply, give permission for them to be released. It could be that you have to take action before they fully leave you, so ask if there's anything that you need to know, or to do, in order to help shift them. And when you're ready, bring yourself back into the moment, back into the room; stand up, stretch and drink some water to help ground you.

If you drink water after this exercise, it will really help your body shift whatever you've released out of your body too.

If you are doing this exercise at night, know that activating the energy centers will activate energy in you, so you might have trouble sleeping. You can visualize a dimmer switch dimming all of the lights in your body once you are happy that you've cleared them. It really depends on your metabolism and energetic make-up as to how this will affect you, so just be aware of this. Perhaps try it for the first time at a different time of day.

After you have done this work once, it gets easier to do, and you will find that you can do it faster, too. There are also some variations that you can try once you become confident. For example, you can breathe in healing energy through the top of your head, all the way down to the center at the base of your spine, then run the energy all the way up your spine, igniting all the other energy centers as it passes by.

This is a big and important exercise. If you think you will have trouble with it, I have created an audio recording to guide you through it step by step. Just visit my website shop, download it, and put it on your mp3 player and you've got it there whenever you need it: http://abby-wynne.com/product/clearing-your-chakras/

It's Good to Talk

We need men to talk more about what it is like to be a man in today's world. We need strong, healthy men to do their inner work, to support each other and hold space for a world where boys can grow up and become strong, healthy men. In this chapter I hope I've helped you smash your idea of what you thought you should be and release the pressure you put on yourself to be something other than who you already are. We need you in the world as your best healed self.

You may need additional support while doing your work so know that there are other men out there who are willing to listen. And if you don't want to talk to a man, there are women out there who want to help too. When you hold things in or lock them away, they become heavy and *you* become heavier and heavier over time too, until one day you wake up and find that you just can't go on anymore … not as you are, anyway. Know that there are ways to heal this. The rate of male suicide in the world is at an all-time high right now, and it's not because men just wake up one day and decide to end their lives. The feeling of hopelessness happens slowly over time through the building up of these heavy energies that are not talked about or healed.

It's time for you to help turn around the culture of silence and carrying pain. I ask you to be a pioneer and do your work: talk to a male friend you trust; tell them what is going on for you. They might not know what to say to you or how to listen to you, so before you even start to talk, tell them, "You don't have to fix this for me. I just want you to listen, to know what I'm going through. I need a friend, someone on my side who knows what is going on in my heart." Once a man knows what to do, it makes his life simpler, right? Take your friend off the hook before you even start talking—have a conversation about having a conversation so it makes it easier for you to talk as well. Knowing that someone else knows what you're going through even though they cannot fix or change it magically alleviates pressure on you, and answers may even come in miraculous ways just because you've put it out to the universe that you need them. That's the beauty of the healing process.

Affirmations for Connection
to the Divine Masculine

Connecting to Divine Masculine energies is something we do subconsciously, so being aware that you're doing it can be empowering. Here are some affirmations that work equally well for men and women, so any reader may change them if needed, to see what it feels like to activate this aspect of the self. Notice your belief percentage; see if there is any work you need to go back and do at a deeper level to increase it to 100.

- I am enough just as I am.
- It is safe to feel all of my emotions.
- I release my anger and I center myself.
- I am grounded and strong.
- I can do all the things I need to do.
- I let go of difficult thoughts and I am nicer to myself.
- I can be strong and have an open, loving heart.
- I connect to Divine Masculine energies and ask for the strength I need to do the things I need to do.

Chapter 6

Your Darkness

This chapter is about the parts of you that you know exist and don't want to admit to: the parts you are ashamed of, unwanted behaviors, addictions, and your nasty side. Everyone has these parts; they are not shadow parts because you know they exist. These are the parts of you that you deliberately keep in the darkness.

Darkness exists and is a necessary part of growth. I will explain this in more detail, and show you how you can accept all of the parts of yourself, to create wholeness.

This chapter is about the darker aspects of who we are: the parts that want us to fail, and the parts of ourselves we recognize and try to cut away. These parts are the ones that are nasty and mean behind people's backs, and hurtful and angry toward ourselves and others. We can have knowledge of these aspects of us and try to shut them out but it won't make them go away.

New Age thinking calls this our shadow side, but I beg to differ—your shadow side is the side of you that you are not aware of. Others could be aware of it, but you aren't or don't want to be. The more you learn about yourself through the work you do and your willingness to do it, the less you hide in your shadow as you reveal yourself to yourself.

"Shadow self" as a term has been used to describe an aspect of ourselves with behaviors we are aware of but are not proud of or happy with, and we usually do not want to acknowledge or talk about it. These are your bad behaviors, the worst aspects of you. Once acknowledged, however, I don't believe we can call these behaviors shadow aspects anymore. I consider them aspects of us that prefer the dark, and we like to push them into the dark so we can get on with our lives.

You have the choice to work with your shadow self to transform it; as long as you're actively working together, this part of you stays in your awareness, hence my calling it "your darkness" rather than "your shadow." What happens when you step away from them is that these behaviors dissolve back into the dark spot of your awareness. Most of the time you would really rather not think about them, and not seeing them allows you to believe that you have healed them, but you really haven't.

Darkness versus Shadow

Many spiritual teachers relish working with shadow; they host shadow workshops and work with shadow behaviors. However, as I've already said, once we know about these behaviors, they're not shadow anymore. We have darkness within us; darkness exists and lightness could not exist without the balance of darkness. It is up to those of us who strive toward the light to work with our darkness, whether it be in the shadows or not. This makes us fully aware and fully responsible for all of our behaviors at all times. It sounds like a lot to ask for, and yes, this is the hardest work of all.

I believe that there are two driving forces we are subjected to: one pushes us toward death, and the other pushes us toward life. Depending on our background, experiences, and outlook in life, we may find that we are more on one side than the other, but we are all subjected to both of these forces from within. How these forces manifest themselves within us depends on our strength of character and our determination to heal ourselves.

There are many facets to the dark side of us, just as there are many to the light side. We see some of these dark facets in people who have overinflated egos, arrogance, pride, selfishness, hunger for power, and greed. When given free rein, that's where true evil resides. People who take pleasure in hurting other people exist, and we would be fools not to recognize this. Some of these people are too far gone to return to center.

Shadow is a real thing. Artwork without shadows is very two-dimensional, as the figures lose depth and substance, seeming artificial in a way. Likewise, there will always be things you don't know about yourself, which are your true shadow aspects. These aspects are not always unwanted or "bad" behaviors—they could also be aspects of you that are maturing and ripening for your discovery when the time is right.

Other people may be able to see things about you before you do. For example, I had a client who for years didn't realize that he was gay and when he eventually did, it took him a long time to accept it. Once he was ready to reveal his true self, he very hesitantly came out to his friends and family. They shocked him with their reaction: "We were waiting for you to say this for years!" Can you relate to this with something in yourself?

Isn't it interesting that the opposite of shadow is reflection? Reflections are what we and other people see. However, when something is in the shadow, we only get a sense that it is there; when something is in the darkness, we may not know that it is there at all. Only when we bring the light of our awareness into the shadow can we see it, and if the only thing there is the darkness itself, the light dissolves that away.

Getting Clear

Before we start, I want to be clear about where I am coming from for the work of this chapter.

There are parts of us that we know about and don't like. I prefer to call these difficult or unwanted behaviors rather than dark aspects of us. There are also parts of ourselves we don't know about so we don't *know* if we like them or not: these are our shadow aspects. Spiritual and personal development teachers have developed a spectrum that places shadow behaviors on one side and light on the other. This arrangement insinuates that shadow behaviors are bad ones, but they're not. They're part of what makes us whole. There are always going to be opposite ends to a spectrum. Our concern is not about the absolute dark and light at each end—it's about how to stay in balance.

The battle we have with the forces of light and dark within explains why we can end up attacking ourselves and wrecking the good healing work we have done. Just as we need to balance masculine and feminine, we need to balance dark and light, shadow and reflection, death force and life force.

It must also be said that we go through periods of our lives that seem to be in darkness, where everything seems to go wrong, but we come out the other end stronger and better for it. And we have periods of lightness where everything seems to be going well, but they do not last forever. Just as winter turns into summer and back to winter again, just as day turns into night and then comes the day, we are part of nature and move within cycles of darkness and light. How the cycles affect you depends on how robust you are and how much work you have done on yourself. Everybody is different.

I cannot emphasize enough that doing your inner work is the answer to getting through these dark cycles. You start to like yourself more, you become a friend to yourself, and your attitude both to yourself and to others becomes more compassionate. You begin to trust yourself more and show yourself more of yourself. This is the creation of the best healed self, the authentic, congruent self, which will prevail in challenges. It is therefore important to do the work thoroughly. As people go deeper inward, they tend to avoid the parts they really dislike or are afraid of. Though those parts are in darkness, they are still there and still need to be healed. That's what this chapter really is about.

Are You Ready to Work with Your Dark Side?

You must do a significant amount of work on yourself before you can be strong enough to really face the darker aspects of yourself. You need a high level of self-esteem so that your responsible adult can continue to hold you strongly when you go into the darkness, even to just investigate it. To be able to name the core issues at work within you and embrace the struggle you're having with yourself is work that frees you up to really be available for life. We're headed to a place where you can be completely on your own side, support and accept yourself totally, and always look after yourself and be your own best friend.

If you haven't done work on the more difficult aspects of yourself and you think you're done with healing, that doesn't cut it anymore—your difficult aspects will show up when you least expect it. Avoiding this work is avoidance of one of the biggest pieces we need to attend to. We need all aspects of ourselves on our side, which is why this work happens after we have, for the most part, embraced our inner child and inner teen, released a wellspring of grief and anger, allowed ourselves to feel what we feel, been present more in our bodies, and at least attempted to balance the masculine and feminine within.

Healing Happens in Layers

This chapter may unlock some of the reasons you may feel you've not gotten very far with the work in this book up to now. It will give you more tools and techniques you can use to go back and redo some work at a deeper level. In truth, we remove layers and layers; it's not "going back," even though you may have to literally turn the page back to chapter 1. What we are actually doing is going deeper. I've written this book with layers in mind, so an exercise you've done lightly in chapter 2, for example, will enable you to do further work in chapter 3. After the work here in chapter 6, go back to chapter 2 and you'll find a new dimension of the work has been opened to you—it will have much more profound healing effects.

It's time to step into the shadow, into the darkness. If you're not feeling ready, that's okay too. Just ask yourself, "What is it I need to do to become ready?" Ask with honesty and wait to hear the answer. It might take a week or a month before you receive the answer, or it may only take hours or days. Or it may take years.

This healing work is about you, so you must take *your* time and *your* pace to do it. Don't rush through it quickly. Healing is not a race. The quality of life you are experiencing increases when you're authentic, when you accept yourself, and when you are free from internal struggle. It is absolutely worth the time it takes to get there. So read on and perhaps something will strike you as not being as difficult as you thought it would be; perhaps even just by reading on, a layer of your work will "unlock" by itself. And if something overwhelming comes up for you, don't hold on to it by thinking you can handle it by yourself—we are not meant to do this alone. Ask for help. It's big work, and by doing this you actually increase your sense of confidence, self-worth, and self-esteem. You owe it to yourself to treat yourself well.

Self-Sabotage

Self-sabotage is when we knowingly or unknowingly destroy the good healing work we have done. Everyone on a healing journey has done this to themselves at one point or another—and many times too. I can admit to this, and I think if you deny that you've done it too then you're avoiding work that needs to be done … which is a form of self-sabotage!

Sabotage can come in many forms, at many different levels. Because you know yourself better than anyone, the saboteur in you transforms as you transform. It is sneaky and clever and can catch you out so that you can even sabotage yourself before you realize that you've done it.

The inner saboteur is more complex than anything we have worked with so far, as it is not one specific aspect of you but instead qualities that are ingrained in many aspects of you. Each part of you that sabotages you needs to be identified in the moment and worked with in turn. Patience with yourself is essential for the work, as is the expectation that something like this does not heal quickly.

I believe there are many reasons why we sabotage ourselves, ranging from the childish to the very complex, depending, of course, on which aspect of you is out of balance. All those reasons have power over us (even the childish ones) as they are real and require our awareness and a compassionate approach. Here are some in no particular order:

- We are afraid to be powerful, beautiful, and healed because we are so used to not being those things and are afraid we will no longer recognize ourselves in the transformation.

- We are terrified of being perfect because when we "get" there, what are we supposed to do next?

- We are afraid of being powerful in case we abuse that power and go around thoughtlessly harming other people.

- We are afraid to be powerful because we will then feel like we have to use that power to fix everyone else and we have no interest in that.

- We are afraid to heal because we think that when we are healed we will forget what it is like to be a human being, lose all of our friends, and be unable to relate to anyone anymore.

- We are afraid to heal something in particular because it has been the go-to addiction for us for many years. Even though we hate it in ourselves, we also find comfort in it and don't want to lose the way it comforts us.

- We are afraid to heal because the last time we were well something bad happened, so we associate the thing that happened with being well, instead of it just being a thing that happened while we were feeling well.

- We are afraid to be healed because everyone around us is suffering so we need to suffer too.

- We are not allowed to be happy because there is deep, underlying anger at ourselves about something we did or didn't do in the past that we have not forgiven ourselves for.

- We are not allowed to be healed because we are not able to forgive someone for something they did; forgiving them would mean that we have to take some of the blame, and we don't want to do that.

- We are afraid that if we become healed we will have to leave our marriage/job/home and our lives will change dramatically. It would be too much to handle, so it's easier to stay unwell.

- We are afraid if we do our work that we will hurt someone we love.

- We are afraid that becoming healed means we have to do work that is so terrifying and horrific. We then become afraid of the work. The fear of doing horrific work builds up and becomes greater than the work itself and we get trapped in fear.

Sometimes it is not us doing the sabotage. Energetic forms of sabotage are real, but I am not going to cover how to deal with them here as they are too big for the purpose of this book. If you resonate with anything in the following list, you may need to get some help to release it. Don't forget to check out the resource list in the back of this book with advice on how to choose a good Shamanic/Energy worker. I have worked with many people to successfully clear their energetic blocks to healing and am available to do work with you too, if you so wish.

- We have inherited patterns from our ancestors that are blocking us from becoming healed. They didn't heal, so they don't want us to heal, and they are energetically in the way of us healing and keep us in a place of disempowerment through our weaknesses.

- You're living in an environment or have relationships with people that drain your energy, and you have no energy to actually summon the strength you need to do your work. (See *How to Be Well* for help with this.)

- You have been cursed/made energetic bonds or vows either in this lifetime or in another lifetime and have carried the bindings into this lifetime.

- You are being bound to a soul contract that no longer resonates with you and need to change the contract and close unfinished business before you can have access to the resources you need to complete the next level of healing work.

Do you have a different reason that is not listed here? Please take some time and read each one again, think about it, and ask yourself, "Am I doing this?"

As the deeper work of the more difficult aspects of you reveals itself for healing, know that you don't need to do anything about it right away, but you do need to acknowledge it, like walking past someone on a country road. Catch their eye, nod your head, and move on. The act of catching their eye means that you know they exist, and knowing that something exists in the dark is the first step to bringing it into the light.

The Work Starts Here

I offer several different directions that you can take with the work of this chapter. They are in no particular order and have come to me via the work I do with clients. I find that these are the most common traps and pitfalls we create for ourselves during healing. Read this as the responsible and rational adult you are, see what fits for you, and try the exercises out if you feel called. Though there is always more work for you to do beyond the scope of this book, this is a good start.

You Will Never Be Your Ideal Self, So Get Over It

We are humans, we mess up. We are designed to do that, and it's in our nature. We forget this when we go on a path of healing thinking that we have to be positive all the time, never swear, never lose our tempers, and never get frustrated. Wrong! We are allowed to swear (I do, lots) and we are allowed to lose our tempers, especially if someone drives into our car, skips the line, or hurts someone we love. As I said, it's how we are made.

Yet, we still hold a vision of ourselves as ideal or perfect. We all do it. This is the *you* you're wanting so badly to become; the "when I am this person, my life will be perfect and I will be happy" kind of thinking. But there's always a gap between where you are now in reality and where your ideal self is (with the slim body, the family, the big house—you know what I'm talking about).

I work with lots of women in groups, teaching them how to empower themselves and to step into becoming their best healed selves. When I started out, I saw how much self-sabotage was going on in all of my groups and I do have to say, it shocked me. The participants wouldn't do their homework, they would wallow in self-pity and they'd go into "I'm not good enough" mode without even realizing it (that's shadow stepping in as the victim mentality). These grown adults would actively sabotage their progress by going on eating or drinking binges, not participating in the work, and reacting to things when they were learning about responding. Afterward I would hear the stories about what happened to them to "make them" do it or what "makes them" the way they are, but between the lines of the stories I noticed the excuses as to why they didn't want to do their work. So I changed something.

The first piece of work we do in my empowerment groups is healing all the blocks to becoming your best, healed, most powerful self. It has made a massive difference in the results. I'd like to do some of that with you here in this chapter now. Are you up for it?

Exercise

How Far Away Is Your Ideal Self from Where You Are Now?

Picture a timeline and place yourself on the present moment. Place your ideal self in the future, at a time when you think that you will be that person.

Now imagine that you're healing and moving forward in time. What happens to your ideal self? Do they wait there for you, or do they move forward in time too?

What amazes everyone who does this is the realization that no matter how hard they work, they will shift and change the idea of their ideal self as well, so the gap will always be there between the two. When they realize that they will never become their ideal self, they realize that it's time to abandon that idea. Being your best healed self is enough, and in fact it's all you can be, so let yourself feel the pressure release and the huge relief around that.

Your Best Healed Self Is a Human Being, Just Like You

We touched on work related to anger in chapter 5 on the Divine Masculine, but I want to go deeper into it here as well. Know in your heart of hearts that your best healed self is allowed to get angry. The difference between someone who is their best healed self and angry and someone who's just angry is the reservoir of carried anger. The person who still has their wellspring of anger that has built up for years and years without release may still have not forgiven someone or cleared emotional pain from their past. They still have triggers inside that activate when day-to-day anger is elicited, magnets of emotional pain inside that attract more emotional pain into their lives. An unhealed person's reaction to something that would make anyone angry can be over-the-top too much, and they can then hold on to that anger for much longer because processing their "today" anger means also processing the depths and wellsprings of anger that lies beneath.

When you've done your inner work and healed the wellspring of anger (see chapter 5 for how to do this), your trigger points are less explosive. Your behavior becomes a response to anger rather than a reaction to it. You are more in the moment and can handle the anger based on what has happened rather than based on what has happened *plus* all the other things in your life that also happened. You are able to clear the anger and ground yourself, focus and have clarity, and come up with a solution that is not based on revenge, jealousy, or anger. You can get angry (and you will), so make space for that. I see anger as a positive creative force that makes you say or do something that you might not have done otherwise. Remember that anger is a symptom that something is wrong: either you feel unfairly treated or you see someone else being unfairly treated. It's all healthy and good unless it festers and simmers and bubbles and boils up in you and makes you sick. That's why I keep saying do your work—don't let it fester!

Healed People Can Get Sick Too

Your best healed self can get sick; in fact, healers often get sick too but recover quicker as overall they have healthier constitutions. People make mistakes but healed people learn from them quicker and are less likely to make the same mistakes again. Your best healed self makes bad decisions from time to time, then realizes what they did and puts it to right. They can inadvertently hurt people by saying hurtful things in the spur of the moment, but they own it, apologize, look into why those things slipped out, and heal it. There is always more healing to do. Are you with me now?

Your Best Healed Self Is You at Your Best, in This Moment Now

With what you know in this moment, you're already at the point of being at your best healed self. Just like you say "I understand that you were doing the best that you could at the time, with what you knew" to others, this also applies to you. You are doing your best right now with what you know. There is always more to do, you know it, and that's still you at your best. Or to put it another way, your best healed self is the responsible adult you already are, only the responsible adult is the master of your life, not the wounded parts of you. The responsible adult in you is authentic and has morals, values, ethics, truth, and love at their core. Your best healed self also has much more fun in life, so it really is worth taking the time to do your inner work.

Replacing Your Ideal Self with Your Best Healed Self

Now that you know your best healed self is allowed to swear and get angry, how does that knowledge change how you see yourself as healed?

Exercise

Tuning In

Have you decided that when you are healed you will also be perfect? Seriously? Is there some childlike aspect of you that holds on to this as a fixed idea? And is another aspect of you terrified of the prospect of letting yourself down because it knows you will never be perfect?

Write down everything you've always aspired to on a personal basis: the house, the kids, the big job, the car, and so on. Write down everything you feel you have not yet achieved that when you do, you'll be happy. No holds barred here—this is for you and you alone, so even if the things you have aspired to are silly, inconsequential, or frivolous, they're in your mind so they have to come out. I've heard lots of these kinds of aspirations: "When I lose forty pounds," "If I had blonde hair," "When I get my degree," "When I get promoted," and so on.

Pick the most urgent and important aspiration. Put the others away for now. Bring yourself into your body more fully; let go of your thoughts, worries, and fears. Just breathe and be with this thing you want, this thing that is in the way of your happiness.

Now imagine that you already have it. So if it's weight you want to lose, imagine the slimmer body inside your today body. Visualize the fat melting away so you are sitting there, slim. Let your energies settle into it and really feel as if you have become slim in the chair, in this moment. Let yourself really feel you have that degree, that house, or the husband and kids in the next room.

Now I'm going to ask you a question: Who are you? It's a difficult enough question to answer, isn't it? I want you to try to answer.

Connecting to the Truth of Who You Are

Here you are, in the energy of the thing that is holding you back from happiness. You've got the sense of what it is, of what it would feel like to have this thing, and you've got the sense of who you are when you have it. Let's consolidate it and bring it into the light.

Exercise

Your Luminous Being

Close your eyes and slow down your breath. Soften your body, let go of tension, and relax. Really feel what it feels like to be present in this exact moment, right here, right now.

You are not your body. Who are you? Imagine that your skin starts to dissolve away, your muscles and bones start to melt away, your internal organs melt away, until there's nothing left but the essence of who you are, the true and pure essence of your soul. This is who you really are.

Feel the flow of the beauty of the energy that you are. Tap into the love that flows through you, the freedom. Know that your personality is what has the facets that are causing you the difficulties; what's responsible for the blocks and fixed ideas are just parts of you but *not* who you truly are. Know that your attachment to ideas and things are just illusions you have created. They're not real, they're not who you are, and you're already whole. Let the need to have this thing—this image of your perfect self, your perfect life—dissolve into the beauty of the flow of your energy. Know that you are enough just as you are, right here in this moment.

When you're ready, you can bring your awareness back to your body. Imagine that your body reappears very slowly—organs, bones, muscles, skin. You're back. Bring awareness to your legs and feet, hips, stomach, chest shoulders, arms, head, and face. Breathe and open your eyes. Can you now connect into that sense of the energy beneath the body, beneath the personality in you? Can you see how you are not your personality, but it is an aspect of you like the inner wounded child or the wounded teen? Is the need still there, or has it gone?

When you feel like you're really back in the moment, get your list out and have another look at it. Ask yourself, "Are these things stopping me from being happy, or is my personality stopping me from being happy?"

There is big learning for many people when they do this; really seeing the personality as a separate thing is actually a big help in moving forward with inner work. To be able to see the other person as a beautiful soul who has a personality with fixed ideas, flaws, and imperfections just like us is also a big help when it comes to relationships, enabling us to love more unconditionally while keeping our boundaries and conditions when interacting with the personality.

Fear of Power as a Block to Healing

We are all powerful, but most of us have a perverted idea of what power is. Power is what makes the car go; force is the will behind the power that directs the car to its destination. It's not the power that you need to be afraid of, it's the direction and force of your will. If you have a car that is all fueled up sitting outside your house, you have the potential to go anywhere, pure and simple. Where do you choose to drive this car?

When you are aware of who you are and live from your heart, power is a marvelous thing—it can help you make changes in your life, help other people, and help yourself. Learning about what fills up your power levels and doing it when needed is very empowering. Setting healthy boundaries, saying no to someone when you don't have the power to give to them can actually be very beneficial to them too, as the quality of what you offer when you're at your best is far superior to what you give reluctantly when you're not. Know yourself, and do what you need to do for you.

It makes for empowering friendships when you can be honest with each other. When you are able to say "I'm too tired to meet you today as planned, can we do it another day?" and the friend responds "Of course! Take the time you need and let me know when you're feeling better," their response helps you. That's the kind of friend you don't need to use excuses to avoid, and it leads to a much healthier and happier relationship.

Exercise
What Does Power Mean to You?

Get your journal and answer the following questions. Be as truthful as you can.

- What does being powerful really mean to you?
- Are you allowing yourself to be powerful in your own life?
- When you have access to power, what do you do with it?
- Who do you think is a powerful person? What are their negative aspects? Their positive aspects?
- What are you really afraid of in you?

Calling Power into Your Life

Working at the energetic level has profound effects at the level of reality. By inviting power into your life, you will see all the things that are blocking your power so you can begin to work with and clear them. When you see your blocks, know that they could be based within aspects of your inner child or inner teen, or they could be related to how you hold yourself in your day-to-day life. The choices you make that disempower you are the manifestation of your lack of desire to hold onto your power because you don't really believe you can handle it. If you set your intention to heal what is ready to be healed first and go gently, you can build up a gradual trust in yourself, so that you eventually move into embodying the knowledge that you *can* choose wisely when you are in balance and living from your heart.

Only do the next exercise if you're feeling truly ready for it.

Exercise

Invocation to Invite Power into Your Life

Say these words standing up strong with your feet on the ground, for it is a declaration, an invitation, and should be said with feeling and strength behind it. Doing this outside in nature where you can speak out loud can be very freeing and allows you to really feel the emotion behind the words.

Don't say this because you feel you have to, and don't say it apologetically. In other words, don't do it in your back garden if you're afraid the neighbors will hear you. You can also say it out loud without shouting. Decide what feels appropriate to you. You can also use the words I give here as a mantra, saying them over and over again to create or solidify a source of power in yourself that wasn't there before.

Spend time with each sentence before you say it, as you might want to alter or change something. Make sure you believe each sentence 100 percent. If there is an aspect of you that doesn't believe, then figure out which one it is, and that's your work already begun.

- I am allowed to be powerful in my life.

- I invite my power to come into my life.

- I ask to be released from any energetic binds that are holding me back from being powerful, both mine and not mine, across all space and time.

- I give my full permission to release anything in me that undermines my self-confidence and power.

- I allow myself to be powerful in my life.

- I step into my power and feel what it feels
  like to be powerful in my life.

- I commit to doing my inner work and clearing
  all that is in the way of my most powerful life.

- I am fully responsible for how I feel, who I am,
  and what I choose in every moment.

- Thank you, thank you, thank you, thank you!

There are lots of triggers in this invocation for you to work on. See this as the opening of your door, the invitation for power to come into your life, and the work you will have to do to get your house ready so that power will want to stay with you. Remember too that you *are* doing your work—learn what your blocks are and how to clear them, and do it. Use these words as a power source, or write something for yourself. We do need to draw on sources of power, and when doing difficult work, power comes in very handy.

The Dark Night of the Soul

Dark periods of our lives are part of the cycle I spoke about earlier. However, it isn't socially acceptable to be in a dark period, and society's mentality is one of fixing, curing, healing, and taking our medicine. Because we are uncomfortable with difficult emotions, we don't honor this part of the cycle for what it is; it's not taught about in schools, and the media and society at large generally frown upon it. It's unfortunate. Anyone I have worked with who has been in a dark phase eventually realizes that it *is* a natural part of growth, and it is therefore okay to not feel comfortable or pleasant because it is part of the process. Overall, this realization makes the pain a little bit easier to bear.

The dark night of the soul is when our reality collapses upon us and we are forced inward to look at our lives, how we live, what we think is important, and what is *really* important. The dark night of the soul is a time to face up to the lies we tell ourselves and each other, the persona we show the world and the person we really are within. In our times now, what is not true needs to fall away; we cannot bear to carry the weight of it. This event can be a very difficult wake-up call for many people. You're here doing your work, so you already know this.

While we are in darkness, we feel lost and give our power away. We are uncomfortable and all we want to do is get the heck out of it as quickly as we can. But it's deep within the depths of the darkness, emotional pain, and burden of grief where we meet ourselves and make that choice to cling to life and decide to stay. Somehow only then can we find the endurance and strength we need to get through. This is growth, and yes, I'm fully aware, some of us don't make it through. The man who felt sorry for the butterfly cut open the cocoon to help, and the butterfly fell out and died because it wasn't finished transforming. If we try to rush through the darkness too quickly, the transformation is not complete, and we may get stuck there or have to go back and do it all over again. But remember that coal is just coal until pressure turns it into a diamond. There are gifts in the darkness, and once you look for and receive the gifts, the darkness moves on.

Depression

Depression is the loss of a zest for life; being depressed brings with it a loss of motivation, a dull emptiness inside—no passion, energy, or desire for anything. It can create total and utter apathy, it can be heavy and crushing, or it can feel like part of you has simply left and you're only half of a person. The most common form of management for diagnosed depression is medication that switches off the emotions and anxieties associated with it.

I believe that most forms of depression are a spiritual sickness caused by soul loss and anger turned inward. There are forms of depression formed by chemical imbalances in the body, and in those cases medication is the correct way to manage it. However, I also believe we as a society are very quick to prescribe medication, thinking that medication is the *only* way to manage depression.

I've experienced depression and have healed it in me, and I have helped others heal and move on from it. It's a complex illness that deserves more time than a section in a chapter in a book, but I'm writing about it here because I want you to know that if you are feeling depressed, there is something you can do about it. We will do a soul retrieval in chapter 7 but you must work up to it rather than jump ahead. On my website are soul retrieval recordings that you can download and listen to over and over again to help you get the pieces of your soul back. I am also available for sessions, so if you want personal help, do get in touch. Some resources that can help you with soul loss are listed in the appendix.

We can become depressed due to excess energy being consumed by solidified anger. If you have tried the "Release the Wellspring of Anger" exercise in chapter 5 and felt that even after trying it you're chipping away at a mountain that keeps growing back when you're not looking, then you need to get some help rather than feeling like you're going to be crushed. If you believe there is no way out, that is what you create. Please hear me: You are not alone in how you are feeling, not at all. Many people experience this and recover from it. There is help—you just need to ask for it, and there is no failing in asking for help.

Addiction: Bringing the Darkness in Upon Yourself

I'm mentioning addiction here because it is a coping mechanism particularly when we are in denial of our feelings. Addiction is a compulsion or a dependence on a substance or activity that is usually harmful to the person in question. I believe addiction is the outward manifestation of something deeper that lurks in the shadows. Addiction is a great distraction, bringing you into the drama and events that go around your poison of choice and away from the core issue. Addiction masks the deep feeling of loneliness when we shut everyone out of our heart, including ourselves.

There are many causes to addictive behaviors because we are more complex than we appreciate, so making and breaking addictions can be a full time job. Going deeper into your addiction is like bringing the darkness in upon yourself, allowing yourself be drawn toward the darkness—it's very alluring, so it takes big power and courage to snap out of it.

I can't give you a magic recipe for healing addiction because I don't believe there is one. Additionally, we all have addictions, even if we want to convince ourselves otherwise. They take many forms and can rank from subtle to devastating. To heal an addiction, we have to want to heal it wholeheartedly, know that most of the aspects of us are on our side, and open our hearts fully to ourselves. Admitting that we have an addiction strips away everything, leaving us standing in our vulnerabilities and our fragility. It is big and complicated work to truly let go of addiction; most of us cannot do it on our own.

How Does Addiction Begin?

When you're running away from something you don't want to think about or feel, there's no better way to do it than to play a game, get lost in a fantasy, or dull the pain with a drink. I believe there are three potential causes to addiction: denial of a situation in life that you don't want to deal with, dulling the pain of feelings you don't want to feel (e.g., boredom, anger, loneliness, sadness), or an inherited energetic pattern that creates a predisposition to addictive behaviors without the need of a direct cause.

Gambling, sex, alcohol, or drugs are the traditional ways we lose ourselves in things and shut down feelings. When they become more attractive than dealing with the feelings, things turn problematic. Somewhere in the progression of attraction, a hook forms between the person and the behavior of choice—a dependency the person feels that, for example, "masturbation is my way out of feeling like this" or "gambling is my way out of this." The person then becomes dependent on their behavior of choice to take them out of facing the work they have to do. Of course in the case of actual substance abuse, the physical body is deeply affected by toxins and there is a chemical reaction that creates a dependency on the drug before the energetic and the mental addiction kick in. At that point the person's energy fuses with the behavior, and it becomes harder to detach the person from the behavior.

How Do You Heal Addiction?

If anything I have said here resonates or seems to be true for you, my advice is to do your inner work. Don't be afraid to open yourself up to yourself completely and look at what you've got left to work on. Use the exercise in chapter 5 with the boxes (It is safe to feel what you are feeling) to allow yourself to ease into what is in the dark edges of your subconscious mind.

The only solution to addiction is to know yourself inside and out and look after yourself so that you don't get lost in it. If you're born with a predisposition for substance addiction, you need to put in extra effort as the responsible adult that you are to grow up and heal the inner child in you so you can look after yourself instead of relishing in the joy of the few minutes away from reality.

Bring your Divine Masculine and Feminine strength into play, and use the force of your will to simply not go there. Connect to Spirit if you're called to do so; call upon healing energies and ask them to release any cravings or need in you. Try the exercises offered here, such as the one in which you dissolve your body away until you are only light. All these things bring you out of your mind and out of the craving, and into a healed space.

Personally, I've never smoked or taken drugs because I know I have that predisposition. However, food has been my drug of choice for years; it took years for me to heal that in me, but I did it. And now that I've cleared the behaviors, the energetic pattern in me has shifted. I've connected deeply to Spirit so I don't feel that ache inside. I feel that I've reached a point in my life where I'm balanced and happy. And you can do it too, if you dedicate your will, focus, and determination to be the best you that you can be.

There Are Benefits to Being a Victim

On reading the title of this section, my editor wanted me to delete it as she thought it was too harsh. I am not blaming, naming, and/or shaming anyone here—I'm looking at what we invest our power in, because what we invest in is what grows. Deciding that you're helpless and a victim is very different from being or feeling helpless, and when you're in a dark night of the soul or a dark phase, you may indeed feel like a victim at times.

What I am talking about here is clinging to your wounding for years and years, giving power to your diagnosis and *becoming* your illness. When you make everything in your life revolve around the pain in your life, you feed it with your life force. The drama, the self-pity, the consolation from your friends and family are like an addiction. The benefit? Not having to function in your life, being the center of attention, and having everyone do everything for you so you don't have to. This way, you avoid having to take responsibility for anything. Maybe you know someone like this.

Even if you're suffering or in crisis, you can still choose to feed the healing process and ride the waves of discomfort knowing they will pass. Reclaim your power and ask for the strength you need to get through whatever it is you're going through. Separate yourself from your feelings, your illness, your diagnosis, and don't become it. It is dangerous to identify ourselves by the pain.

Just like the healed self is allowed to feel anger based on whatever happened now (and not about all the other things that happened in their lives in addition to the thing that just happened), and let it go relatively quickly, we can step into feeling like a victim for a time, as long as we eventually move on. That time is relative—it might take years for some, weeks for others. But if we strive for the light, we feed the light, and endure no matter how long it takes to heal; we move forward. Every day we heal a little bit more and give the healing our focus, not the pain.

Some people don't move on because there are benefits to being a victim (this is shadow behavior) and if the person is aware of it, one of their dark aspects in action. I believe calling attention to this is important because we can slide into lazy shadow behaviors because it's easy to do so. Depending on your life situation, choosing to be well and heal doesn't always mean you will be cured. However, you can *always* heal something, even if you can't see it with your eyes.

Being the Responsible Adult Is Too Scary

What is it about responsibility that scares people? How do you feel when you say the following out loud: "I am fully responsible for how I feel, for who I am, and for what I choose in every moment."

It's great to sit back and blame everyone else for everything. Are you doing this in some form in your life? Regarding the victim mentality, you *did* make a series of choices in your life that led to whatever situation occurred that you're now blaming someone else for. Yes, maybe they are at fault, but are you aware of all of the choices you made that brought you to that moment? Then perhaps you are also at fault.

If you want to be in your power, you need to take responsibility for everything you do or don't do, say or don't say, or even think. Own it.

Exercise

Journaling

Answer the following questions:

- What does being responsible for my own life actually mean?
- Where in my life am I not taking responsibility for something?
- What am I afraid of when it comes to being responsible in my life, for how I feel, for how I behave, and for what I choose?

Remembering that your best healed self is allowed to make mistakes makes this a lot easier. Know also that you are not responsible for how other people feel what they choose or have already chosen, and that no matter who they are, is it not your job to heal them. You can be responsible and decide to take a day off work and sleep because you really need it. You can be responsible and realize that you've taken on too much for you alone, and ask for help with it. But thinking that you can handle things yourself when you can't is making a bad choice for you, and your internal saboteur could be at work, ready to tell you "I told you so!"

Here's the thing—nobody made you do anything; you chose to do it, for whatever reason. So own that. Maybe it was a bad choice, but you're the one that made that choice. Track back the situation to understand the energy you were entangled in that led to the choice that you're not proud of, and untangle that energy so it doesn't happen again. That's the learning, that's being responsible. Track back in your mind to the time and place you made the choice you're not happy with and learn how you became disempowered, learn what your weaknesses are, and empower yourself by healing them. Knowing your shadow tendencies and your weak areas is part of becoming more aware of who you are and what you are choosing. Rather than getting angry at yourself, learn how to make better choices and not get entangled with your weak spots and strengthen them. Make a plan for the next time you might be in a similar predicament. Ask yourself, "What do I do next time in this situation so it doesn't happen again?"

Being Responsible for Our Own Feelings

Nobody "makes" you feel anything; the emotions you feel are a result of experiences you had, the wellspring of emotions you already carry, and the thoughts you have about yourself. You are responsible for what you think. For example, what you think of yourself when you're grieving can affect your grieving process: "Is it too long? Not long enough? Just the right amount of grieving? Is there a right amount of grieving for the loss of [a dog/parent/child]?" Now your mind is telling you what you should be doing—or are you just allowed to feel whatever it is that you're feeling?

When you're at peace with yourself, you allow yourself to feel sad if you're feeling sad. Most of us don't do that; instead we accuse others: "You made me feel ..." But they didn't, not really. The other person triggered you and *you* felt it yourself. Giving someone else control over your emotional state is like giving them a remote control to your inner world: they press happy and you're happy, sad and you're sad, angry and you're angry... It doesn't work that way at all. I'm sure you've experienced someone wanting to make you angry at some point and they just couldn't pull it off because you were in too good a mood. And maybe because you felt good that day, you didn't say something to them about your boundaries that you thought you should have said after the fact. Being aware of how your mood and levels of emotion affect the choices you make is also good work that you need to do.

You Are the Light in Dark Places

It is important for you to understand that you don't need to be sad around sad people so they feel better, and in fact it doesn't make them feel better because you can't make people feel anything, remember? Being sad around sad people just adds to the levels of sadness already there. See yourself as a light that shines in the world, and as you clear your wellsprings and accept yourself, learn who you are and become more at peace with yourself, your light shines brighter. Being a bright light in the world reminds other people that they can also be a bright light, stimulating them to do their own work. You aren't saying, "Look at me, I've done my work and *you* have not done yours." You're not bragging—you're just being you in your wholeness. Other people's shadows might not like that and it might affect your relationships with them, your light may bright out their darker side, but this is a risk you have to take—stay stagnant and keep the peace and be unhappy with yourself... or grow and shine, and disrupt a few people's shadows while you're at it. They'll settle down, or they won't. It's up to you to decide if you're going to make this a point of self-sabotage too.

You might not be ready to go gung-ho into this work, but you can still say to yourself, "I know that I have to do some work on my victim mentality, I'm just not ready to do it yet" and that brings it straight out of your shadow. Ask yourself what you need to do in order to prepare yourself to tackle the victim aspect of yourself, or whatever other aspect of your dark side that you've decided to heal. Ask yourself if you're ready to take the risk with the other people in your life who want to remain as they are and see your healing as a threat to themselves. Ask yourself with compassion and love, listen to your answers, and ask for the help you need. As I always say, go gently.

I give lots of help with how to do this type of transformational work in *How to Be Well*; it's a great companion book to this one. It covers disempowerment, how to get your power back, how to be more aware of your choices, and how to master your emotions in the moment. It also looks in more detail at how your healing affects the other people around you and ways that you can handle it.

Different Types of Self-Sabotage

In this section I'll briefly look at a few different forms of self-sabotage. You can see if they resonate and if they do, add them to your list of work. These are by no means the only forms of self-sabotage, and if you don't find yours in here it is worth taking the time to figure out what your go-to sabotage pattern is so you can heal it. Just by asking a really well phrased question, you set the wheels in motion to receive the answer from your inner wisdom and from your higher self/future healed self. Start asking and you'll see what I mean.

Procrastination versus Laziness

I once worked with a woman who was in her sixties who cared for her husband who was in his seventies with Alzheimer's. She was very upset when she told me that she had managed to organize respite care for him for a day. She had lots of things she planned to do that day to catch up with administration of the house as well as some errands. She ended up spending the whole afternoon staring out the window, doing nothing. She was distraught; she called herself lazy and cried. When the emotion had passed, I told her that she was in fact working full time, as even at night in her sleep she was still available to her husband. That day was the first day of freedom from being on call she'd had in several months, and she needed that space to catch up with herself. She *needed* to look out the window all afternoon; she wasn't being lazy at all.

We are so quick to accuse ourselves of being lazy, but it isn't always about that at all. For example, I have found over time that when I have a to-do list and don't want to do something on it, I usually find something else to do instead, and the feeling of not wanting to do something at a certain time is actually a reading on the energy of that thing and can actually be quite a good thing, because it will either work out better at another time, or it wasn't meant to be at its originally planned time. I have a great saying: "Divine timing is not always our timing." It's not an excuse for not doing things; it's more like an invitation to work with intuition as well as the logical side. Maybe you relate to this?

You are allowed to be tired. You are allowed to put things off until a different day and time. You are allowed to drop the ball, so to speak, as long as you pick it up again. And you are allowed to change your mind and not do something you were going to do. When I told my client that she needed to rest and make sure she got more regular breaks, she saw herself in a different light and stopped being angry and upset at herself. We can only do as much as we are able to do.

When we purposely distract ourselves in the hope that the task will disappear or that someone else will do it, that's the shadow at work, the sabotage aspect. It consciously or subconsciously tells you that not doing something you know you need to do will make it go away. When this happens to me, I ask myself what I need to do for me that will make the job easier to do rather than attack myself for being lazy. The question is useful to ask, as there is usually something that wasn't taken into account.

So book your dental appointment and go. Visit your uncle and tell him you love him. Ask yourself what is stopping you from doing your task, and deal with it so you can do the task. The pressure that builds up by ignoring the task or pretending that you don't have to do something eats into your power. It drains you. So stop it.

Taking on Other People's Emotional Pain

Many people are wired to be caregivers, and though we looked at the caregiver child in chapter 1, it does need to be mentioned here as well. One aspect of the caregiver who is out of balance is taking on other people's wellsprings of pain because they feel they can handle them better than the person who is carrying them, as if they are saying, "I'm an expert at being sad, so give me your sadness because I'm better at dealing with it than you." When we take on others' emotional pain, we disempower them. When we try to fix other people, we disempower them. And the real reason we want to take on others' pain is because seeing them in pain is too painful.

From the goodness of your heart, when you as caregiver take on their pain, it means they will not do the work they need to do to learn the lessons they need to learn. In essence, you aren't helping them, and you're sabotaging yourself by carrying more emotional pain than you need to.

Be with the idea that you're not God: you don't get to choose who is in pain and how they handle or don't handle their pain. Become comfortable with your own pain so that you can look at other people in pain and not become devastated and upset by it. The enlightened woman looks at the advert for the charity that helps starving children in war-torn countries and says, "My inner wounded child is starving for attention, which is why I have so much trouble watching these adverts." She knows her weakness, is compassionate with herself, takes responsibility for it, and (hopefully) does her inner work. Alternatively, imagine the therapist who has not explored their own inner workings and while listening to a client in distress one day, becomes deeply triggered by the client's story and cannot contain their own emotions. The effect this can have on a client is incredibly damaging—imagine that person talking to a friend after that session saying, "Even my therapist thinks my situation is horrendous! They were bawling and crying when I told them what happened to me."

Know that being able to listen to someone who is in pain without stepping into their pain and feeling it too is much more helpful to that person. They don't feel like they have to mind you because you're upset for them, and they feel safer to offload in a place where they know you won't take it on. Their pain will clear and heal faster that way too.

Saying Yes When You Should Be Saying No

Another aspect of caregiver sabotage is when a caregiver gives away more energy than they have because they don't want to hurt someone's feelings by saying no to them. People do this for a couple of reasons: they don't want to cause other people emotional pain, but they also do not want to take responsibility for themselves, their choices, and their energy levels. The best way to work with this is to know that you do it and then to learn how to read how much energy you have so you can use that to make better choices rather than say yes to everything.

Exercise

How Much Power Do You Have Right Now?

Imagine you are a car and personal power is your fuel. How full is your fuel tank right now? Don't answer from the top of your head; your mind would like to think you're in better shape than you actually are.

Slow down your breath, come into your body, and ask your heart, "How full is my personal power tank right now?" Get a picture of it in your mind. Is it half full? Two-thirds full? Say thank you to your heart.

Then breathe, slow down again, drop down into your stomach, and ask your stomach the same question. Are you getting similar answers between mind, heart, and gut?

Knowing how full your tank is gives you something to work with when it comes to taking on too much. When you visualize how full your power levels are, you can't claim you didn't know and can instead use this as an indicator that some self-care and nourishment of your power levels is required. There are lots of loving and compassionate ways you can say no to things, so learn how and set good boundaries.

And here's the real kick up the you-know-what: as the overzealous caregiver, you don't get the "thank you" you are expecting from those in pain whom you've helped or decided to "fix." In fact, they probably don't even realize that you're working so hard for them. Your inner shadow caretaker becomes resentful of the other person for not appreciating you and all the work you're doing. But as we've seen in this chapter, you're not really doing it for them—you're doing it for *you* to avoid doing your own work. So stop it.

Fixed Ideas About Things Not Based on Truth

Both caregiver sabotage patterns here are actually based on fixed ideas that are not true. We all have limiting beliefs about ourselves that hold us back. And just as with the reasons people sabotage themselves and don't heal, some of these ideas are quite childish and others are real—and *all* need to be healed. Here are some more examples of fixed ideas, some conscious, some subconscious, all of which hold back the healing process and cause internal sabotage:

- A particular person is angry at me/mean to me/jealous of me so I need to stay away from them to protect myself.

- A particular person is needing my help because they can't do things by themselves, and even though I don't want to help them, I really have to do it.

- I am not good enough and I don't deserve it so I might as well not even try.

- I am better than so-and-so, and *I* should be the one getting all the attention, not them.

- I can't be around or allow myself to feel emotional pain because I will fall apart.

- If I say no to someone it will hurt them, because someone said no to me one time and it really hurt me.

- If I am powerful in my life, I will become a mean, nasty, angry person.

Refer to the list at the beginning of this chapter for more. Do you know what your fixed ideas are? Can you catch yourself when you work out of them? Can you work with yourself to change them? You heal this when you know what your fixed beliefs are, which aspect of you holds them so tightly, and you create a space to talk to them as the responsible adult with compassion. Know that whatever aspect is at work here is anxious and has some reason to hold on to this belief, so work with them and ask the question you need to ask: "What do I need to do to help you let go of this belief?" See where you go with the answer.

Active Destructive Addictive Behavior

A woman signed up for my Heal Emotional Eating Bootcamp: 21-Day Online Class because she knew it was an issue for her. She did all the lead-up healing work, the journaling, and the group clearing, yet she went on an eating binge in the middle of the course. She was terrified to tell me what happened, but she was brave and took responsibility to tell me. She was surprised that I congratulated her for telling me, as she assumed I would be angry and was so relieved that I wasn't. I told her it was wonderful that she was aware of what she did and that I believed the forces that pushed her into destructive behavior were too strong for her to fight. I suggested that instead of being angry and upset that it happened, she could connect into a source of love and compassion for herself. She could forgive herself for not being strong enough yet to fight the destructive forces within, but she knew that if she kept going, one day she would be strong enough and heal this in her. The exercise I gave her to try appears later in this chapter.

Our destructive pattern starts in the shadows, possibly based on a limiting belief, but it is no longer hidden from us once we become aware of it. Then we have awareness but don't have control over it. Once we realize we need to heal it, we can then make the decision to heal it … but that doesn't stop the pattern; it only shifts it slightly. It can take years to shift patterns like this, particularly when the behavior is an active, addictive one that brings a sense of comfort to some aspect of ourselves. We subconsciously become afraid to heal this because it has been the go-to addiction for us for many years. Even though we may hate it in ourselves, we also find comfort in these addictions and don't want to lose the way we are comforted, even if it's just short-lived.

When you focus on the comfort you get from this type of behavior rather than the discomfort, you realize that you must fill the need the behavior is trying to fill with a healthier alternative before you're able to let go of this behavior. We need to find comfort from something else before we feel safe enough to let go of the unhealthy form of comfort—this is how you successfully break addictive and self-destructive patterns. You are required to have great love and compassion for yourself, which is the opposite of the self-hatred that most people feel while in the pattern of it. Love breaks the pattern. Love is what heals.

Healing Self-Sabotage When Your Power Has Split Off from You

I will end this chapter with the most powerful work you can do to bring yourself back into wholeness.

To recap: Power is not good or bad, it is what you choose to do with it that is good or bad. So if you have a death wish against yourself and are afraid to be powerful in your life, it's probably a good idea to look at what this death wish is before you go any further. Being so angry and hateful toward yourself doesn't come from nothing—there is always a reason behind it. What is it you're angry about? What can you not forgive yourself for? Do you want to heal and become your best self, powerful and happy in your life? Do you want to be that light that inspires others to shine? Did you find the true core limiting belief that is holding you back? This is the most powerful battle you have with yourself, and you will try so hard not to go here, but you have to if you want to heal.

When an aspect of us does not want the thing we are striving toward, it can kick up, act out, and wreck everything. We have already looked at this kind of reaction in many ways, but we have not looked at sheer power as a separate aspect. When split off and angry, your personal power can be a scary thing. Maybe you've heard people call this part of themselves "my inner demon" or "the monster that wants to destroy me." Putting power into form—a visible shape or configuration—so you can work with it is actually the first step.

During a residential shamanic workshop I attended, I sat on the steps with someone one night and we allowed our inner "monsters" to go out and wreck the place while we sat on the step and supported each other to stay sitting there. It was an amazing experience to feel that the monsters inside us could emerge to act out on their own rather than acting out through us. We sat there and described what was going on to each other as if we were describing an imaginary cartoon scene in front of us: our monsters were saying nasty things, throwing furniture around, drinking too much alcohol, and fighting... but our physical bodies sat on the step while it was happening. Eventually our monsters burned off the energy they needed to without hurting anyone else or each other... and we survived it! Both of us felt like we had mastered some part of us that didn't want to be tamed. We felt so free to know that we didn't have to go drinking, say nasty things to each other, and get into a fight in this reality but our energy got what it needed: recognition, space, and time. It changed something for me forever.

When clients come to me with a similar sort of energy that's active in them and I ask them to put a form to it, they see this energy as a demon, monster, or gargoyle. Dobby the house elf from Harry Potter is a popular form to pick for this energy, as is Gollum from The Lord of the Rings. Some people realize that this inner saboteur is in fact themselves, and they create the form as an aspect from a time of their lives when they felt really unhappy and disempowered. The biggest mistake people make is to try to split, kill, or run away from this part of themselves or replace it with something else that's nicer to be around. Unfortunately, that only makes the power more powerful and *also* angry. The energy then behaves as if it's in a pressure cooker, waiting for a good time to explode. Instead, I invite these aspects into session to get their point of view. Once they're invited to speak and be listened to, something changes. Just like the other aspects of you, this one also has a case to make, an argument to share. They have needs too. And usually the need is to be listened to and allowed to have a say, even if they're angry at you.

Connecting to a Source of Love and Compassion for Your Inner Saboteur

The intention behind this exercise is to connect to love and communicate with the parts of you that seem to want you to fail, those difficult parts of yourself. You know at this point that you cannot lock these negative aspects up and hope they disappear— they are part of you and must be taken with you. Decide that you are able to do so before doing this exercise, and then read through the exercise before doing it, making sure you're feeling strong when you do it so that you're the one in control.

Exercise

Connect to Compassion for Your Inner Saboteur

Make a space where you won't be disturbed. Slow down your breath, relax, and come into your body. Because you are facing the most difficult parts of yourself here, you might need some support while doing this, so play some music in the background, have a crystal in your hand, or have a trusted friend hold you safe and in a loving space in their mind's eye for a set period of time. You're the responsible adult in this exercise.

Connect into a source of love and compassion for yourself. Feel the light of compassion connect into the top of your head, into your body, into your heart, up and across your shoulders, down your arms and out your hands, into your stomach, down your legs, and into the ground. Feel your heart lighting up with love and compassion for yourself, for all the work you've done, for all the work you are going to do. Breathe in compassion, breathe out stress, and let your energies expand so that you are more present and contained in the moment.

Close your eyes, and when you're ready, go to a safe space in nature. Let the images come to you. Look around you: Where are you? What is the weather like? What is around you? Let yourself settle in and become comfortable. Remember to continue to breathe in compassion and love, let your heart light shine out, and feel grounded and safe.

If you need some help to meet the shadow aspect of you, ask your angels, guides, or a power animal to come. Ask your future healed self or a loving, helpful ancestor to stand beside you.

Allow the part of yourself that is so angry at you to show up here. This is the nasty devilish or demonic part of you in whatever form it has taken. Allow the part of you that is consuming your power to step in here. Just be with this part of you without saying anything. Just get your bearings with it.

When you're ready or when the shadow aspect is ready, have a conversation: What does it want from you? What have you forgotten or neglected to do or to be? Listen to the truth of what is going on. Just listen.

When it's your turn to speak, remember all of the discussions that we have had in this chapter, remember all the learning that you have had on your healing journey, and calmly offer solutions to your shadow part. Say what needs to be said, and ask questions to find out more. You're the therapist for your shadow now, so you need to listen deeply, *and* it also needs to listen to you.

See this part of you soften as it realizes that you are serious and want to heal, that you care about what it has to say, and that you don't want to leave it behind but embrace it as part of you. It might shrink or become fuzzy and cuddly, or dissolve away and become part of you. Take note of what happens here, because this is the first time you've done it. It won't stay soft and fuzzy if you don't do what you say you will do to keep it happy.

Give thanks to your shadow part and ask it if it will show up for you in this form or in the original form. Ask also if it has a message for you or if you go off track and need a reminder to do something in the context of what you have discussed. Make an agreement to work with your shadow part instead of having a battle with it. Tell your shadow part that you intend to have fun in your life and that it can help you be the whole person you are.

If you feel able to hug, do so; if all you want to do is shake hands, then do that. Do try to come to some level of agreement before seeing your shadow part dissolve away, leaving you and your guides in the space in nature. Well done.

Now, ask for healing—you've healed part of yourself by having the conversation, so let your guides and angels heal you now with showers of light, however it looks: jump into a lake and swim, bask in the sun, whatever you want to do. Take some time in the landscape to feel like the pressure and anxiety have left and you've regained a part of yourself you had forgotten about. This part is beautiful and will help you in the next stages of your healing journey.

When you're ready, come back into the room.

Take some time to sit with what you have learned; you might need to do this work a few times to really have a breakthrough. If you've been avoiding your inner saboteur for years, they might not even show up. Keep coming back and making yourself available so that trust builds between you. Do whatever it is you said you'd do for them just as you would do for the other aspects you've already been working with. You've got this.

Accepting All Parts of Yourself, Even Ones You Don't Like

There are lots of stories of Jesus Christ but only one or two of them are about him losing his temper. My daughter told me that she didn't like Jesus because he seemed too good to be true. I told her that just because there were no stories of Jesus coming home, slamming the door, throwing his bag on the ground, and having a good rant about how crap his day was doesn't mean that he didn't do that. People tend to only talk about the things they want to talk about, not the whole of it. The more I thought about this, the more true it seemed to me: if Jesus was a real person, he had his faults, his moments, his shadow, and his darkness. What do you think?

We need to do our inner work and embrace the difficult parts of ourselves so that we become whole, not just people who are "good" all the time. We can't be "good" all the time anyway; we have to let off steam and process our anger because we are alive here in this world where we see and experience injustice all the time. It's easy to be enlightened when you live on a mountaintop away from everyone. Like Ram Das says, if you think you're enlightened, go spend a week with your family. If you're in any type of relationship, prepare to be triggered!

Knowing that you're allowed to be angry and frustrated takes the pressure off. Knowing that there are parts of you that you probably don't like but will learn to accept is part of this work too. We are perfect in our imperfection.

On my shaky and weak days (and yes I do have them) I look after myself more and/or ask for help instead of being angry at myself. I work with my eccentricities rather than struggle against them. For example, sometimes I wonder whether I locked my car, so before I leave it I say out loud, "I have locked the car" and sometimes take a photo of the parking space so I know that I'll find the car again, which is much better than getting upset and angry at myself. Some days I just want to stay in bed, so I look at what is going on and make some time and space to rest. I also occasionally eat a guilt-free chocolate brownie, simply because I don't make myself feel guilty over it. I work with all aspects of me, not just the ones I want to present to the world. All the aspects of me have reached an agreement together, and it's wonderful to be completely on my side and not have an internal struggle every day. The peace is indescribable, and I wish it for you too: to know, accept, and work with yourself, not against. You don't have to present yourself in your totality to anyone, but you do have to step out of the shadows, shine a light on your darkness, and present your whole self to you.

Chapter 7

Your Light

When we clear our inner emotional pain, dissolve away fear and anger, and become our best healed selves, there still is work to do. We still need to look after ourselves, fill ourselves up, rest, contemplate, make mistakes, learn, and grow. Life is an obstacle course that can knock us sideways, so working with our light can keep us centered and balanced if done on a regular basis. For as long as we are alive and engaged with life, there is always more to learn.

Why is there a chapter about working with your light in a book about healing inner wounds? "Surely," you think, "working with the light is the absence of wounding … the place we are aiming to get to, yes?" Well, just like cleaning a house, turning on the light reveals a whole new layer of work to do, and I would be remiss to not mention it to you.

The light I speak of in this chapter is your inner light, your zest for life, the glow you feel when you are well. It is the light behind your eyes, the light inside you that shines outward it is your vibrant health. This light comes from the pure radiance of your consciousness—when you feel good, you're a bright light, and you inspire others to shine brighter too. It is your motivation and will to take action in a specific direction. The affinity for love, justice, honor, and truth are the light seen in peoples' eyes that kindle it in our own. When you are happy and feeling the freedom of being completely who you are, it's the light you shine out into the world. Feeling "lit up" about something can make you hyper and out of balance; it's the mania to the depression and can trigger your shadow and make you feel invincible when you're not. Therefore, it's important to know your limitations and be able to work with all parts of the spectrum.

There are ways to feed and nurture your light that I want to talk about here, and there are also downsides to being clear and vibrant in your energies that need to be discussed. But everything is manageable if you're aware and learn how to manage it.

We all have access to light and it plays a role in our lives depending on who we are and how we are made. When our light shines, it reminds us of the truth of who we are as opposed to the stories we tell ourselves. Everyone brings light into the world by shining their light as pure and clear as they can, all the time, every day.

If you're an empath or a healer, you have the framework within you to bring even more light into the world. Lightworkers are people who actively work with light, helping people shine their own lights brighter, healing the land and its plants and animals actively through healing practices, or simply by being there. Lightworkers can devote their whole lives to purifying and expanding their light and helping others do the same. It's a New Age misconception that if you have this ability you must hang a shingle outside your door and see clients. You don't. Healers heal just by being present in the world. So if anyone has ever told you that you're a healer, then just by shining your own light as best you can, you're already doing all you need to do.

You might not be a lightworker, and that's okay—it's not a job for everyone. Your job is to shine *your* light as best as you can. This happens naturally when you are well and happy, and being the best you can be. Whether you are a lightworker or not, dear reader, know that we all have darkness and we all have light, so this chapter is relevant to all. Here I will talk about a deeper level of spirituality, how to maintain your levels of lightness, and how to keep dark and light in balance. Know that you don't have to be religious to be spiritual. Read this with an open mind, watch what triggers you to see if there is more healing you need to do, and don't hesitate to review previous work to enhance your process.

Just as with any chapter in this book, all the exercises I offer you are an opportunity for you to learn how to shine your inner light that little bit brighter and how to heal yourself. We have been working with healing light since the beginning of this book, so nothing here will feel brand new; only the context has changed. If you try some of the work here, you may be amazed at how easy it is to access pure healing light and how beautiful it can feel.

What Exactly Is the Light?

We all have a body, a mind, thoughts, and emotions. Your consciousness pours into your body, mind, and emotions. Some parts you are aware of (consciousness) and some you're not (subconsciousness). We have looked at how to work with both parts in previous chapters and have looked at different aspects of you that are actually aspects of your consciousness—again, some you were aware of and some you were not—but perhaps you are more aware of those subconscious parts now after doing healing work.

So where does the consciousness or life force that is "you" come from? Your life force is pure consciousness, so it has to come from somewhere, doesn't it?

The pure source of all universal consciousness is a much greater entity than our capacity for comprehension could ever handle. It's a bit like asking a first generation computer to create a full length animated 3-D movie—it's impossible! The computer I had in college didn't fully load up even after I went and made a cup of tea, and my smartphone now has more capacity than that computer ever had. When you consider that our brain is hardwired for fear and survival, you realize that it's not really designed to understand love and light at the degree to which we now have access.

With the limits of the mind taken into consideration, we can grasp why humans have never been able to come to an agreement as to what the source of all universal consciousness is, and in fact there isn't even a name for it we can all agree on! Many wars have been fought and lost, and many people have died because people have wanted ownership of the what, how, when, and where of the source of all consciousness, but Source has no rules—humans do. That said, there are laws for Source akin to the laws of physics. Laws in this sense are different from rules, as you don't need to understand or even know about the law of gravity to be affected by it. The miracle of Source is that it can break these laws at any time, should it choose to do so.

The source of all consciousness has been named many things: Allah, God, Great Spirit, the Universe, the Creator, to mention a few. Source exists beyond whatever we choose to name it, and it is not limited to whatever object of worship or faith we happen to believe in—it is also the source of your inner light. It has a vibration and a frequency (based on the laws I mentioned), so it's not simply energy but energy with consciousness—divine healing energy, Reiki, prana, chi, whatever you'd like to call it, it is unlimited in its potential.

How the Light Works With Us

I see the configuration of body and ego as a container for consciousness; ego is the principal through which we organize ourselves in the world based on our emotions, beliefs, experiences, thought processes, and whatever we choose to invest our personal power into. You could call it our personality, if you want. Like power, ego is neither good nor evil. Ego is a structure for our consciousness that enables us to live on planet Earth and interact with the environment and each other. As we heal, ego softens and expands. When we refuse to heal, ego hardens and constricts. The amount of consciousness that flows into our container (ourselves) is limited depending on its structure, which is based on how much pain we carry and how much healing we have done.

Imagine your emotional pain is a blanket and your inner light is a table lamp. When you hold on to emotional pain, your blanket gets thrown over the light, and the light shines through it but is dim. Over time, if you don't heal and remove those blankets, the lamp becomes smothered. And as you heal and remove your blankets, your inner light seems to shine brighter because you can see it better.

Recall one of the reasons we sabotage ourselves from chapter 6: "I can't heal when the other people around me are suffering." Know that removing these blankets and allowing your light to shine reminds people that they can remove their blankets and find their own inner light too, just like you did.

An actual table lamp is connected by a wire and a plug to a source of electricity that lights it up. Your inner light is connected to the source of all consciousness. We forget this, however, as we focus on our blankets and the other lights around us and cannot see the wire or plug that is connecting us to Source. We have to learn to believe we are connected and learn how to actively use our "plugs" to connect and get a flow going. If you have ever seen the movie *Avatar*, you would have seen the Na'vi plug themselves into a neural network to communicate with other beings on their planet and receive pure Source energy. We can connect to the source of all consciousness in the same way but it's more difficult to do when we don't have an actual socket or plug and we don't know it's there.

The more the emotional pain, the dimmer the lamp, but things are not always so straightforward, and the lamp dimming does not always happen in a chronological way. You could imagine that severe trauma could smash someone's lamp or diminish its power to that of a dim night light. Or consider that someone else's lamp is not made like yours, and something that has little impact on you can have a massive impact on them. Depression could be when the lamp is totally blanketed, the plug and wire totally forgotten, and no light shines through. Importantly, *the light is still there*—it's just more difficult to see it.

Exercise

How Bright Is Your Light?

If your inner light were an actual lamp, how many blankets are covering it? Let your subconscious mind show you rather than you deciding from your conscious mind.

Ask yourself about the wire and the plug: When was the last time you plugged into Source and felt the power surging in you lighting you up? Would you like to experience that now?

Ask yourself what is in the way and listen to your inner wisdom.

I believe that science will never be able to calculate or measure the immensity of consciousness. I also believe that our brains will never be able to comprehend the full complexity of who we are and how we are made, and possibly the full truth of why we are here. All we can do is make our best effort to purify our container so it can hold a higher quality of consciousness and connect to the source of consciousness to increase our flow and brighten our light. We leave our container behind when our body dies, but I believe the quality of our consciousness doesn't die—it moves on to another realm so the work we do in this life is never lost.

Expansion

When we work with the light, the quality of our container (body and ego/personality) improves and expands, and over time it can hold more light of a higher quality. You could liken this phenomenon to upgrading a lamp; you would work with a wire, a plug, and a light bulb all attached to the electricity. The power of the electricity going through the wire is the voltage, and the thickness of the wire dictates how fast the electricity can travel through it, the flow. So when you have a wire that can handle more electricity with less resistance, your light bulb shines much brighter. If you turn the electricity up too high and the bulb can't handle it, it bursts. And like that light bulb, sometimes a similar thing happens in spiritual situations where you overdo it, which can shatter your container. Balance and capacity are very important.

If we upgrade a physical wire, decrease the resistance, and use a stronger bulb, we can increase the electricity's power and the light will shine brighter. Likewise, when we do our inner work (upgrade our "wire") and let go of emotional pain (decrease our resistance), then more consciousness (power) naturally flows into us and our light shines brighter. We can't control the power flowing from the source of all consciousness but it seems to know exactly what we can handle at any one time. So when we do overdo it and our light bulb shatters, it's not Source energy that shatters us, it's our negligence.

Living Small Makes You Small

When you move through the world in emotional pain, angry and with fixed ideas, expectations, and attachments, you become tight and small, and your energy body shrinks. You cannot access large amounts of life force energy (light) and you have a low tolerance and snappy temper, and your body can get sick. You can also become small in your energy if you are disempowered, feel threatened, or are living in survival mode most of the time.

In contrast, when you release emotional pain, and release your attachment to always being right, your energy body expands. When you free up your energy from the things outside you and become empowered, your energy also expands. More life force can come in, and your body can heal itself. The shift from being a small presence with a low level of life force energy to an expanded one affects not only your energy body but your physical, emotional, and mental bodies, too.

Your idea of who you are and what you are capable of matches your energetic size—you feel and think small when your energy body is small; you're caught in the details of everything and go around in circles with it, you walk with small steps and look down at your feet, your body is hunched over and muscles are tight, you grumble about small things most of the time, everything makes you angry or anxious, you're always looking to blame someone, and you compare yourself to other people and get angry at yourself. It is not a pleasant way to be.

As you do your inner work and release and heal your trauma and pain, your energy body expands. To match this, you let go of details of situations and release stress from being tight. You start thinking bigger, your physical body relaxes, your muscles soften, you stand up taller, and you can see the world around you. You have more self-esteem and enjoy life more, and you are grateful for what you have. You look outward and are able to support and help other people with grace and compassion. Life no longer becomes all about you. You become creative, laugh more, and allow yourself to be seen without the fear of someone not liking or approving of you. Doesn't it feel much better?

The flow of light within someone small is so faint that they may not even register it. I have worked with a few people in sessions where I brought lots of light into the healing room but they felt nothing. It didn't mean the healing was not working; it was as if they had a thousand blankets covering their inner light. If we could remove even a hundred of them in one session (which is a lot) their inner light would seem exactly the same to them.

Similarly, the amount of light received increases as the energy body expands. There is readjustment required in the shift from small to big, and you don't want to shatter your light bulb. The light can be so bright that it reveals layers within that feel painful when they dissolve and let go. These layers reach down to the cellular level of DNA not only within the person themselves, but all the way to past lives, ancestral pain, and beyond. This is work that many healers can do with you, and it's better to get help with work like this than to try it yourself. Read "Choosing a Therapist and Therapy That's Right for You" in the appendix to help you decide what to do if this is something you believe you need for yourself.

Being Your Best, Healed Self

There are not many people alive in the world right now working at their full capacity in the light. I'm speaking of the people who radiate pure light and have a top-of-the-line container and an immense amount of Source light flowing through them at all times, not just when they're feeling well. But we are human, and if we live surrounded by people, we will always be subjected to heavy energies.

Some people can be clear, bright lights for a few moments or a few days but can't hold on to it for very long. Again, our natural relationship with light and dark is best thought of as a cycle: dark to light to dark again. However, we can increase the quality of the light we carry and be more at ease when we are in our times of darkness. Some people are gifted to us to show us the way to what is possible and where we can go with the work we are all doing. When I met Amma, I knew immediately she was the embodiment of pure unconditional love. I could feel her inner light five minutes before she entered the event hall where I was waiting for her. She radiates light for miles. I believe people like this are direct gifts from Source to remind us that we can all do this. We are helped and encouraged to do our work.

If you do the work, heal and remove those blankets of pain you're carrying, and upgrade your container, there will be moments when you feel that mystical connection with the source of all that is. Though these grace-filled moments defy logic and measurement, they are very real: seeing the sunlight illuminate the sky and forgetting yourself completely and becoming the light, too; watching a flower grow and for a moment, you are the flower experiencing *you*; releasing the tension in your chest and feeling totally held and loved and just knowing with certainty that you are not alone.

For now, think about what that connection means for you and what it triggers in you, and then try the next exercise. You can look back to chapter 6 to see if any of the reasons for self-sabotage resonate with you when it comes to standing tall and being bright and big in the world. Do some work with those reasons and their sources if you need to. And know that your work is a process that doesn't happen in a straightforward way. There is a back and forth, setbacks and challenges and tests—it doesn't happen overnight.

Exercise

Removing the Blankets and Connecting to Source

Breathe and relax. Settle your body as much as you can. Sit with your feet flat on the ground with open hands and relaxed posture. You might want to do a healing heart journey in preparation (Journey to Heal Your Broken Heart in chapter 3) or sit in stillness if you're able.

Now visualize yourself curled up in a ball with your heart light aglow. Is it soft or is it strong? If you want to shift the image of you curled up to you lying down on your back, does that feel better? Once you lie down on your back, what happens to your heart light?

Visualize yourself covered by blankets so that you feel the weight of the emotional pain you're carrying right now, in this moment. These blankets don't cover your face but they do cover your body, and in turn, your heart light. Your heart light can shine through some of the blankets, but as you imagine more and more of them, the heart light seems to be dimmer. Know that you don't need to name what the pain is or where it came from—you're just getting a reading on yourself so you know how much work you need to do.

Just by reading this book right through, you've already released lots of your emotional blankets, so allow your mind some time to appreciate the work you've already done and let the number of blankets rise and fall in your mind until you settle on a number of them.

Ask yourself how many blankets are on top of you right now as a way to quantify this work. Know that you will always have a few of them and life will happen. Even your best healed self will need blankets from time to time. By doing your work, you release them.

Now focus on your heart light and give yourself permission to expand and carry more light. How does that feel?

Feel your heart light growing, and as it grows bigger it grows channels outward and downward, so there are now two channels growing down and out each leg, one channel growing outward for each arm, and a channel coming through the top of your head.

Breathe and let the flow stabilize the image so you come into balance with the light coming through you from your heart. Feel it in your physical body as you work with your imagination so you can feel the light opening in your chest, coming down your arms, and out your hands. Imagine your palms glowing. Feel the light as it goes down your stomach to your hips and down your legs. Feel your feet glowing. Feel it as it radiates upward through your neck and face, and out the top of your head.

As you stabilize in this image, notice if some of your blankets change texture, weight, or density, or if some dissolve.

Now see the cords that come out of your feet anchoring themselves into planet Earth.

See the cord that comes out of your head like a wire for a lamp with a plug on the end, and imagine that you're plugging into Source. Take as long as you need for this and when you feel it, you'll recognize that you've been doing this already in most of the exercises throughout this book.

Ask yourself what you need to do to increase the flow of light from Source into you.

Breathe in the light from Source, disconnect your mind from the images of blankets, cords, and plugs, and focus on how your actual body feels right now in this moment. This is where we are; this is where we stay. You don't need to go back to that image. Bring yourself more and more into the room but don't lose focus with your connection.

Feel your feet on the ground and breathe in that light from the top of your head, into your heart, all the way down your body. Do this for three to five breaths. Let your body soften as you do this; it's not about deep, strong, big breaths—your breaths can be natural and soft. Your focus is your awareness of the connection to Source and drawing down more light with every breath. Take baby steps with this, as you might get light-headed. Check your anchor cords at your feet: you might want to sink them deeper into the earth or make bigger anchors to hold you.

Let go of the breath, and bring your awareness to your energy body. Notice how it has softened and expanded. Let yourself fill up the room, just glow in it, receive the healing, and be at peace.

Purification

As you upgrade your container and can hold more light, you may find that things in your life you've always had around no longer fit. Speaking personally, my life has changed so my body has changed too. I cannot tolerate certain foods anymore and have had to change my diet, eliminate toxins from processed foods, and completely let go of sugar. Beyond my diet, I stopped watching soap operas on TV, only listen to the news once a day, and I don't like having the radio on. I have let go of old friends and made new ones, I have different hobbies and habits, and I cannot tolerate hate speech and people venting anger just for the sake of it. I know a similar shift has happened for many of my clients and friends who do their inner work and expand as well.

I believe that this adjustment in habits and behavior is related to the frequency and vibration of the light that you hold: you purify yourself, the quality of your light changes, and so what you are attracted to changes, and what you invest yourself in becomes more important. It's not just food that affects you either— whatever you read, listen to, and spend time with affects your vibration in a similar way. It's inevitable that you're going to have to spend time with people you no longer resonate with, or doing things that make you feel like you've been contaminated; as I've said before, we are human and live surrounded by humans so it is going to happen. If feeling pure and clear is important to you, there are things you can do to maintain it. I always recommend a daily spiritual practice to connect into your spirit and the light directly as well as the practice of cleansing and clearing heavy energies you might have picked up from day-to-day living. Also don't forget to purify yourself with healing Source energies.

It's important to get the balance of purity right—you can't cancel your whole life because you're afraid to become "unclean" —that's your shadow talking. Just as you wash your face and hands and brush your teeth every day, you can create a habit to wash away the heavy energies of the day.

Your Feelings Are Not Always Your Feelings

Jung's collective unconscious is a space that holds all the archetypes (personality types), symbols, and instincts of humanity. I see this space like a deep lake where all of our consciousness pools and mixes together, all of us can access it, and it speaks to us in our dreams. It's as if we dip in and out of it, taking what we need from it. We are not only linked together through the collective unconscious but also through the collective subconscious. Our collective consciousness works a bit like the internet: we are all connected and in motion like a neural network, actively touching each other, drawing information from each other, feeling each other's energies.

The more light that flows into us as a collective, the more sensitive we become. Likewise, the more work we do on ourselves (purification), the clearer we become and the more information we can receive about other people. Like checking Facebook because you think someone has replied to your status update only to see their reply, or picking up your phone a second before you receive a text. Knowing when someone is telling you only half a story and having the sense that something is wrong before you're told about it is another way we can tell we are connected to each other. Think about your life since you've been doing your work: are things like this happening to you more often?

When we are more connected and more sensitive to others, the challenge is not only what we do with the information we receive and how to interpret it but also *how* the information is received and how to tell the difference between what is ours and what is not. At this stage, it's easier to feel other people's feelings, so if you're always feeling the same feelings, your brain will tell you that you're angry again or that the anxiety you're feeling is your own but this is not always the case. For example, if you suddenly become aware you're playing the comparison game or the jealousy game and it's not your thing anymore, you can catch it and tell yourself, "This isn't mine. Please go away now, thank you." Simply knowing that the anxiety you're experiencing isn't yours dissolves it away almost immediately before you get caught up in it.

When you catch yourself in an emotion that's overwhelming, notice it, acknowledge it, and ask yourself if it's yours or someone else's. Gently pull yourself out of it if you need more clarity, know that it's not your fault you're feeling it, and reassure yourself that you don't need to feel these emotions anymore. If there is cause in your life that triggers the emotion, deal with it when you're feeling more grounded and levelheaded. If the emotion isn't yours, see yourself separating out of the collective consciousness like stepping out of the ocean, and see yourself surrounded by a ball of light in whatever color you need in that moment. Really envision yourself stepping away, and allow the emotions to subside.

Doing this at your conscious level is important, and once you've experienced the relief when you do it, your mind will be happy to help you see that you've fallen into a sea of anxiety (or whatever emotion the weakness is) and will help you step back out of it again.

Purification Exercise

If you'd like to bring the light you have access to deeper within your physical body, this is a great exercise to try. I find that when I'm feeling heavy it helps me release stuck energies, and when I'm feeling disconnected, it brings me back to my center. It could also be used as a daily spiritual practice.

Exercise

Bringing Light into the Dark Places

Breathe and bring your awareness into your body from your head to your feet.

Ground yourself deeply in your body, then go through your feet, down the cords of light to your energetic roots and anchors, and check your roots are holding you strongly. Adjust them if you need to.

Connect to the light. You can do this by imagining you're tuning in to a radio station that plays the frequency of healing light or that you've got a cord at the top of your head that you're plugging in to Source energy. You could also imagine that the sun is beaming out a ray of light and touching you. Let your imagination help.

Drop your awareness down your body using your breath, bringing the focus of your awareness into your body more. Breathe in the light, breathe out any heaviness, and open your chest. Do this step several times until you feel you have a flow of energy entering you.

Imagine that your awareness is a torch that lights up wherever you shine it. You are going to bring your awareness deeper into your body now. You are going thickly and strongly inward between your internal organs, behind them, into the cells, the spaces between the cells. Stay as long as you are able at each point listed if you like—this is only a guideline for you to follow, so use your intuition. If your body is ill, see it when you focus on it in your mind, receiving the light to heal and become well. Start with your brain, weaving the light in and around all the gray matter, the folds, and the surfaces in your mind. Bring it down now to your throat, "see" the light being swallowed, clearing and cleansing everything in its path. Come into the chest and see the light in between your shoulder blades, muscle fibers, bones, connective tissues. Feel the light entering your lungs, the complexity of the lung tissue, lighting up around your heart, the bones in your rib cage, shining out from inside you. Visualize the light in your intestines, lighting up your belly from the inside. Shift down to your root, colon, the darkest places where you hide. Bring the light in there and allow any emotional pain you've still got stored in there to be released.

Where else would you like to bring the light?

Sit and enjoy the feeling of flow in your body. Give
thanks for the connection and the experience. Take
your time before you go into the next thing in your day.

Your Soul Is Made of Light

We may never know exactly how we are made, how we connect to each other, or exactly what Source energy is. What we
do know is that we are made of life force energy, a pure light of
consciousness that somehow fills the container that is us. Things
happen over time, such as the trauma and wounding that led you
to this book. Likewise, parts of your soul can leave you because
they cannot bear the pain. Perhaps you've experienced it—something happens that shocks and hurts you and you just don't feel
like yourself for a long time afterward. Sometimes these pieces of
soul do come back when they feel safe and trust that you're able
to mind them (in a very similar way to gaining trust with your
inner child). Sometimes these soul pieces hang around you and
watch you but don't actually come back for good—you might get
flashes when you feel that spark of beauty but then it goes again.
Sometimes you have to go talk to them, negotiate with them,
ask them to come back, and give them what they need in return.
This process is called soul retrieval.

In some traditions, soul retrieval doesn't include asking the
soul piece what it wants, and in fact the practice is quite harsh
because the soul piece must be captured, as if it isn't ready to
come back but has no choice in the matter. Soul pieces retrieved
in this fashion don't hang around for very long. I prefer a more
compassionate and loving approach. It's better to get the soul
piece back in bits and pieces over time that stick with you than it
is to get the whole thing back in one go only for it to leave again.

Because you've done a lot of work and been through a lot even in just the reading of this book, pieces of your soul that may have left in fear may now be ready to return to you. It's time to get them back.

Exercise

Simple Soul Retrieval

Create a space where you feel safe and won't be disturbed.

You're going to go on a journey into your inner self, visiting a forest and collecting the pieces of your soul you have lost for whatever reason.

Close your eyes, feel your body soften, come more into your body, feel your feet on the ground.

Bring your awareness into your heart center, then visualize the most beautiful, magical fairy tale forest you can.

See yourself in there, walking around, exploring. Use your senses and take in as much information as you can. This is the magical forest in your heart, and you can visit anytime you want.

Find the soul retrieval tree, which is there just for you. It's a beautiful, safe, big old tree that looks a little like a hawthorn. On the branches of this tree are magical ribbons, one for each soul piece you have lost over time. Spend some time coming into balance with this so that the tree can show you how many ribbons are there at this moment in time.

Meet the guardian of the tree. The guardian's form can change at any time, ranging from a wise old forest spirit, to a spirit animal, or even an angel. This guardian spirit is kind, gentle, loving, and only wants the highest good for you.

Ask if you can take back some of your soul pieces. Your guardian spirit hands you a basket for collecting the ribbons, and then steps out of the way so you can spend some time with the tree.

To take back a soul piece, touch a ribbon and ask it to come back to you. See it come away easily in your hand. You can now place it in your basket. With each ribbon you feel a little bit more present in the world, a little bit more solid, a little bit more like you.

There may be some ribbons that are not ready to come home to you just yet, and that's okay. You may have some work to do in order for them to feel safe enough. Consult with the guardian spirit of the tree and ask if there is anything you need to know.

Now sit at the bottom of the tree with your basket in your lap. See the ribbons swirling around and creating a ball of energy. They merge, disappear, and now you're left with the energy ball. The basket disappears too.

When you're ready, allow this ball of energy—your soul pieces—to merge with your energy field. Feel them enter your body so you embody them.

Stand up and move around a bit. Give thanks to the tree and the guardian spirit. Maybe you want to jump into some water to wash off any emotions before you come back to this reality.

Breathe and feel your feet on the ground. Bring your
awareness back to your body and the room you are in.
Well done.

You will have to do this exercise a few times to get used to it.
Each time, you will see a different number of ribbons on the tree
depending on the layer of healing you're working with. Some
soul pieces will stick right away and others will disappear again;
either is okay.

I've often found that daily life can wear you down by wearing
away parts of your soul. This exercise is a gentle, loving way to
retrieve those parts so you feel whole again.

Expansion Exercise

When the world is wearing you down (even after a soul retrieval), it's probably because you're doing all the right things,
but are still hiding your magic from the world and from yourself.
You are a creative being, but are you being creative? What makes
your heart sing? What brings you joy? What lights you up?

We also have a tendency to give our power away to other
people, places, and things. We invest our life force energy into
things outside of ourselves and feel bereft when we give too much
of it. We shrink, go back to small thinking, and forget who we
are. But once you allow yourself to see who you truly are, the relief is immense. Stop shrinking for a moment and remember how
beautiful you are. Try this exercise right here in this reality, wherever you are in this moment. Visualize it as you read.

Exercise

Unfolding to Reveal Your True Energetic Self

Imagine you have beautiful wings you have clipped, tied, or bound because you're afraid to be seen for who you are, right here, in this reality. Now breathe and relax and tell yourself it's okay to release and stretch your wings, just for a moment or two. You may need to take some time to convince yourself, but it *is* worth doing this. (If you need to, tell yourself that nobody will see you—it'll just be you.)

As you relax, maybe just imagine your wings start peeking out. Feel your chest open and relax, and allow your spine to straighten up just a little bit. As you get used to the energy shift, you can let your wings unfold even more. If this doesn't work for you, ask yourself if you feel safe right now. If you don't, what do you need to do to fix it?

Returning to your wings, let them emerge. Ask yourself what type of wings you have. Are they butterfly wings? Fairy wings? Angel wings? Shake them out gently now, and notice how your body relaxes more when you let them unfold. Unfold them as much as you can. You're supposed to be here in your full beauty and glory. Can you feel the relief when you do it?

As you unfold your wings, see yourself standing up taller and breathing easier. Your energy body stands up higher than your physical body, so how tall are you now? Take up your rightful place in the world. Can you feel it?

Spend some time unfolding and opening, connect to the light and breathe it in, visualize those wings healing, smoothing, stretching, strengthening. Flap them if you want! Go on a journey with them—see yourself flying off somewhere. Just remember to come back the way you came.

Come into balance with your physical body. Remind yourself that you are this big when you are relaxed and at ease. Notice how big you are so that you will also notice what things in your life make you small, to remind yourself that you don't have to live that way.

When you're ready to move on, you can tuck your wings back in again to go back to the "real world," or not, depending on how you feel. Feel your feet on the ground.

You need to let these wings out to stretch from time to time so you feel better and remember who you are. With wide and outstretched wings, you feel like the creative being that you are. So if you had trouble doing this exercise, try it again, maybe a few times until you get used to the idea that you're safe doing it. You might need to create a space around you with nice music or some incense. I love to do this exercise outside surrounded by trees. Feeling the trees around me gives me an extra sense of security, so I can really unfold and feel safe outside of the noise of the city to stretch out my energy field and breathe.

Make the Light Work as Real as Possible

What you put in is what you get out. Staying connected to the light when all around you is darkness is a feat of intention and willpower. But what if the darkness around you was an illusion?

The Source energy we connect to can be elusive at times, even though it's vital for a lightworker. Making your energy work a habit and making it a real, important thing means that you are less likely to skip it.

Sometimes you get tired and simply need the comfort of something real to hold in your hand. Sometimes it's an Epsom salt bath that cleanses your energy field, or gentle yoga movements, or tai chi. Explore what works for you. And don't hesitate to book a session with an energy healer you trust, as they can help you release stagnant energy and reconnect to your light. It's important to have people around you to support you as you do your work. Get to know a good healer when you don't need them so they are there for you when you do.

Listed in this section are some ways you can support yourself with energies that are palpable, here in this reality. Some may resonate, some may not. Read on for ideas and see what calls to you.

Prayers

Prayers change you, you change things. People get confused with prayer and think of God or Source or the universe as a parent who will make everything better, hence all the begging prayers said every day. However, we made the mess we're in, so it's best to pray for the strength we need to fix it, and perhaps some guidance too.

The actual words and sounds of prayers create energetic tracks that pull down light. The more people who say a prayer, the more worn the tracks become, and the quicker the energy comes. The power of prayer has nothing to do with religion and everything to do with the purity of the intention behind the words and the experience of feeling the energy they bring.

Certain prayers, including the Lord's Prayer (Christian), the Shema (Jewish), and Sanskrit mantras like the Gayatri mantra, have been the fast track for me to feel the connection to Source when I feel energetically heavy and need some light. The first time I said the Hawaiian *ho'oponopono* out loud, I felt the energy come in very strongly. Another time, I felt a profound connection and deep emotion the first time I said the Peace Prayer in the Bhagavad Gita, XVIII. When I read a beautiful poem, my heart opens and I feel the same connection as when I hear a beautiful piece of music. All of these things are prayers when they connect us to Source energy. I believe these particular pieces affected me because of how I am made, the matrix of my being. Perhaps they will work for you, perhaps they won't; you won't know until you try. I write prayers now and share them with followers on Facebook, and my coloring book *A–Z Spiritual Colouring Affirmations* has twenty-six prayers in it, each one with a mandala. I'm continuing to write prayers, too, because I feel the energy of the combinations of the words I choose pull down more light for me and the world.

What is your prayer? Have you ever thought of writing or saying one out loud? When you connect to Source, the energy you *are* is the prayer. One of the most powerful prayers I have worked with is just one line: "Come Holy Spirit." Repeated over and over again, it has a vibration to it and pulls down the energy of Source.

You vibrate at the frequency of the essence you are, and it's all embodied there: fears, anxieties, doubts, and your capacity for love. So when you lose yourself in prayer, forget the present moment, and let the energy of the words of a prayer fill you with

Source, you dissolve the doubt and fear and let in the love. It is a purification. Purify, and your light becomes stronger. This is one way to work deeper in the light.

Your Body as a Temple

If you're eating heavy, sugary, processed foods, they are weighing you down. There are so many chemicals in our food now, and they are in the most unexpected places too. Chemicals clog up your system and stop your body from metabolizing as it should. This is common sense. If you want to improve the quality of light you can carry, you need to improve the vessel that carries it—purification, purification, purification.

You might not realize this but certain "healthy" foods can also block the flow of light through your body. It's a personal thing, as your body chemistry/makeup/affinities/allergies will dictate how this works for you. For example, even though bananas and oats are generally considered healthy foods, for me they are fine in moderation but in large amounts clog me up, as do corn and tomatoes. I need to keep an eye on my food; when I don't, I notice the difference. You will only learn what these foods are by experience, however they're probably your favorite foods, but I hope for you that they aren't!

To bring light into form, eat foods that are filled with light, such as fruit and vegetables, which metabolize the light. In the summer it's easy to get your hands on fresh, vibrant fruits, but they are not as readily available in winter. Food that is filled with light and created by light has light to give to you. Pineapple, nectarines, and watermelon are my favorite—they're light in my stomach and they fill my soul with joy. The preservatives in the winter's dried fruit outweigh the benefit, however; it's best to stick to seasonal fresh food.

What do you like to eat that fills you with joy, agrees with your digestion, and fills you with light? Notice how your moods are affected by the energy of the foods you eat and how what you get out is related to what you put in. If you treat your body as a machine, garbage in equals garbage out. Perhaps an upgrade in the quality of food you are eating will have a massive effect on your energy levels, frame of mind, amount of light you carry, and overall sense of well-being.

Connecting to a Sacred Space on the Land

We all love visualizations where we go to the forest or to the beach; these places help us feel safer to do our energy work. Sometimes you need to bring these kinds of visions into form in our reality by going to a real forest or a real beach. Make the effort, take the time. To where are you called? Where is that tree you love, or the beach that can carry the big emotions when you cannot? These places are important for you to go to regularly in real life, so you can go to them in your journeys and really connect to them energetically.

All land is sacred, and when we have sacred connection with a specific place, it's very special—the energy of your love and attention feeds the energy of the land and a bond is created. There are sacred sites in the world that have powerful energies of their own, such as Uisneach or Lough Gur in Ireland, Glastonbury or Avebury in the UK, or Machu Picchu (Peru) and the Camino (Spain), where people go regularly on pilgrimages. There is a reason people go there, and I personally have received great healing from places of power. Mother Earth has energy lines running through her and wants to help us heal. So take out a map and see what's close to you where you've never been before and where you'd like to visit, and make connection to the land there. Once you've done that in real life, you can feel the energy connection when you journey there and it will further support you in your soul's development and growth.

There's nothing like having a photograph of somewhere you're connected to as your desktop wallpaper or on the lock screen of your phone to remind you that you are held and loved.

We All Need a Daily Spiritual Practice

I cannot say it enough times: we all need a daily spiritual practice. Just as you like the clean feeling you get after taking a shower, you also need to have a spiritual hygiene practice that you do on a regular basis.

How to Be Well has a whole chapter about how to create a daily spiritual practice, and there are many options and varieties of things that you can try, including meditation, mindfulness, and healing, all in a step-by-step, practical way.

I also run a bi-annual online program called "Raise Your Vibration Bootcamp," which I designed specifically to support people in creating new habits with a daily spiritual practice. I work with specific group energies, so each time I run it it's different. Check out my website if you're interested, I'd love to have you join me (www .RaiseYourVibrationBootcamp.com).

You could also use any of the exercises from this book that appeal to you as a daily practice. Take the time to slow down, connect into your mind, your heart, and your inner wisdom and ask your-self what it is that you need to support yourself on a daily basis.

Using Energy to Heal and Balance Your Energy

I have learned that energy affects me in both positive and neg-ative ways. For example, when I'm in a client session where dif-ficult emotions are released, I know that the heavy energies of grief and pain can linger around me and affect my mood unless I clear them right away, so I do it without fail. I also know that I need to meditate every day but some days (as a mother of four with a busy schedule) I don't get to do it, so I need a quick fix that can hold me over. Here are just a few things I do myself; see if you want to try them too.

I use incense, attuned room sprays, candles, and homeopathic remedies as often as I need to help balance my energy. There are ones I don't like and ones I love; it took time to realize which were which. Each scent or variety has its own energy and can help or hinder you depending on what you need in the moment. Invest-ing the time and effort it requires can make the difference be-tween coming home stressed and angry or relaxed and tired.

Like many people, I also use crystals to support me. Each crystal has a vibration, message, or something else to support me on my journey. I have many crystals in my office, on my window ledge at home, and beside my bed. I think of crystals like vita-mins—there are certain vibrations in a crystal I may need at cer-tain times, and I just know by what I am drawn to. For example, popular crystals include amethyst for connection, rose quartz for self-compassion, clear quartz for purification, and red jasper for grounding. The higher the quality of the stone, the higher the quality of the energy. I find that the quality of the stones also reflects the quality of the energy of the person you buy them from, so you need to shop around, be discerning, and always cleanse and clear your crystals before you work with them. I make healing crystal bracelets, by tuning in to the energy of the person that wants one, feeling into the imbalances, sending healing there, and then creating the bracelet to support them as they embody the healing. I call them "prescription bracelets" because the stones have medicine in them, and they're also pretty and fun to wear.

I use music as energy to balance and support my energy, which is a practice I've noticed more clients are doing as well. I use certain music to clear a room before working in it; it harmonizes the frequencies and uplifts the vibration so when I go into the room, it feels much better. I use music to help me clear heavy energies when doing something else, and I use music to help me connect to Source if I'm feeling particularly distracted. I also use music to help me connect to joy—sometimes rock and roll is just the thing to clear stagnant energy in the room! Spotify has lots of tracks in its database, and you can easily make playlists that are easily accessible on your mobile device to help.

The Biggest and Most Important Piece of Work of All

I've saved this for the last exercise of the last chapter because you won't be able to get the most out of it unless you've done some clearing and healing on yourself first. The more work I do with people and myself, the more I come to believe that the most important piece of work we can do is to heal ourselves so we can become able to receive love.

We cannot truly give love when we cannot receive it and feel it for ourselves. Think of offering an empty pot to someone: there's plenty of space in there for love and the theory is great, but the love isn't there—the pot's empty. And if you're an empath or a lightworker who has refused love for yourself, you know that you won't ever offer an empty pot to someone, so you offer yourself instead. You pour yourself into that other person so they are fed and full, and you drain yourself and become resentful.

When you receive love, you open. When you are open, you can contain more love. When you contain love, you spill out love into the world. That's why you need to be able to receive.

Exercise

Release the Barriers to Receiving Love

These are like prayers or mantras: each statement is medicine with power that only works if you say it out loud and mean it. There is a visualization in the middle to help you do the emotional work as well. Read the whole thing so you get an idea of where you are going with this, and allow yourself to take many days, weeks, or months to come into balance with it so you can embody it. I know you will not be able to say each statement out loud and mean it the first time you try this, so be honest and authentic with yourself. Simply stop on the statement you are having trouble with and work with it and the ones before it for several days until something unlocks in you. Then come back and try again until you hit the next one. It's a process.

I am safe.

It is safe to be in the world.

I feel safe.

I bring myself into the present moment completely.

I am here.

I slow down and bring my full awareness into the present moment.

It is safe for me to be here, in the present moment, completely.

I ground myself into Mother Earth and feel her beneath my feet.

I feel solid and strong with Mother Earth beneath me and Father Sky above me.

When I feel Mother Earth and Father Sky supporting me, I can unfold.

I am here in the present moment, and I am held and I am safe.

I open my heart to receive the love that is here for me.

Visualize your heart as a house. What does the house look like? Is it warm and friendly with flowers in window boxes, and a wide open front door, and in full color? Or is the house in dull colors, boarded up, with shutters nailed closed and the front door and gate surrounded by barbed wire? Listen to your heart: What does it tell you? Ask it what you need to do to soften it and let it relax and open to a pure source of unconditional love.

I am here in the present moment, and I am held, and I am safe.

I open my heart to receive the love that is here for me.

I give my full permission to let go of any barrier to pure unconditional love that I have knowingly or unknowingly created across all time and space and dimension throughout my life or in any other lifetime.

I open my heart to receive the love that is here for me, and I release all that is in the way of this.

I release all the blocks I have created and ask for all the blocks I did not create to also be removed and released if it is for my highest good.

I give permission to receive the pure unconditional love of Source with every fiber of my being.

I give permission to receive.

I allow love into my life.

I breathe in love.

I breathe out all that is not love.

I breathe in love.

I breathe out all that is not love.

I am love.

Conclusion

When you do your inner work, you know it. You need to take the time to validate what you have done and mark the occasion so that you can say "yes, I really did this."

This is a big book in the sense that the work in this book is big work—in fact, it's your life's work. It's possible to spend ten years doing the work suggested here. You most likely won't take that long; you're human and life will pull you away from your inner work, which is just fine. I'm not suggesting you stop your life and concentrate on healing yourself. Work like this goes in cycles; you can multitask from time to time, but other times you just don't have the energy for it. Life will go on and you will get caught up in it—it's inevitable.

This book, and the work offered within, is here for you, and I sincerely hope that you find some peace, some solace, and some relief from it.

Ceremony is a marker in space and time to honor an achievement and to give reverence, gratitude, and thanks for the process and the miracle of life. When you feel you've done a big piece of work, you need to honor that and yourself, too—after all, you put the work in. Honoring yourself is not about bragging or wanting justification; it's about you coming into balance with what you have done, validating it, embodying it, and marking it.

Ceremony can take the form of sitting in stillness and reverence for where you have come, emptying out all your fears and doubts, letting go of the image of the small self, and allowing the enlarged self to come out and stay out to become your natural way of being. In this place, your vibration is one of confidence, stillness, peace, and love. If you send a note out to the universe, the note of the essence of who you are, it might sound like this:

> I accept myself completely, I am unapologetic for who I am.
>
> I am my best healed self, and I am learning how to love myself more.
>
> Thank you, universe, for supporting me in my journey of growth.
>
> I see how far I have come and rejoice in it.
>
> I am grateful for the opportunity of this life.
>
> I walk in beauty, I breathe in love, I am the light.

If you like, you can mark the occasion with a gathering of friends —you see yourself anew and want to present yourself to them in your entirety. It sounds a little bit like a coming out party and there may be a risk that someone there won't recognize you and get upset that you're not who they thought you were. They may get upset with you even if you don't have a celebration—hold on to the vibration of the work you have done, remembering that your light shining brighter will remind them that they can shine theirs brighter too. And if they don't like being shown how much work they need to do by being reflected off of you, it isn't your fault, so don't take it personally.

I'm not going to give you a step-by-step ceremony because if you're ready for it, then you are able to create it yourself. Creativity and decision-making in themselves are part of the growing up process, so I hand the responsibility of making decisions for yourself over to you!

Even as you are now, it doesn't mean that you can't receive guidance or chat with a friend, but ultimately this journey is about the healing of the fragmented parts of you so that the responsible adult is in charge, at least most of the time. This is a nudge to you that you need to celebrate the work you have done to receive the validation you deserve. So if you're ready for it, do some research on ceremony and see what you enjoy and what resonates. Don't do what you feel you *have* to do—do something that is meaningful to you. Simply lighting a special candle and saying thank you could be enough, as long as you are fully present to it. I have listed some books in the resources section that can help you get ideas for a ceremony.

Where To Go from Here

Resources are listed in the appendix that can help you go deeper into the work. If you have this book and a copy of my first book, there is enough work to keep you going for years. There is also plenty of support on my website from me, if you want it.

There is always more work to do, and once you answer your calling and step into the light, do your inner work and become the best you that you can be, you will no doubt find new challenges that throw you off balance, and new aspects of you that require your attention.

Never give up. Find your tribe, people you can talk to who will support you as you move forward. Spend time doing things you love; life isn't about working for the money. Connect to your heart often, connect to Source.

Connect to Mother Earth. Our beautiful mother would love you more than all the biological mothers who ever gave birth to you in all of your lifetimes, if you just let her into your heart.

Namaste.

Recommended Reading

You can heal yourself and then harness the power of the energy around you to create the life you've always wanted. Don't take my word for it—go read what these other people say and try it for yourself! Here are some of the books that have helped me on my own healing journey; not all are self-help books. What follows are some of my favorites, and there are lots more out there too. Choose something that resonates with you and see where it brings you.

Bianco, Margery Williams. *The Velveteen Rabbit.* Originally published in 1922 by George H. Doran. New York: Harper-Collins, 1999.
—This beautiful children's story is heart opening and magical. It is a wonderful book for the teaching of values.

Ellis, Albert. *How to Stubbornly Refuse to Make Yourself Miserable About Anything—Yes, Anything!* New York: Citadel Press, 1988.
—A key book in Rational Emotive Behavior Therapy, helping you work with mental patterns to reshape them into something healthier for you.

Gilbert, Elizabeth. *Big Magic*. New York: Bloomsbury, 2015.
—A wonderful book about creativity, ideas, authenticity, and creative living.

Hay, Louise. *You Can Heal Your Life*. Carlsbad, CA: Hay House, 2004.
—Reviews the different parts of the body and what it means when there is illness, disease, or blocks in them.

Hobb, Robin. *Shaman's Crossing*. New York: Harper Voyager, 2006.
—The first book in a trilogy in the genre of fantasy; pure story, but within it is healing, nature, shamanism, connection, soul loss, magic, and hope. Myth and legend play a massive part in the healing process and can unlock many doors in the subconscious mind. I recommend all of the books in her Elderling saga, but that's a personal choice. If you wanted an excuse to read them, however, you could say they're an exploration of values.

Ingerman, Sandra. *Soul Retrieval*. New York: Harper One, 2010.
—A remarkable book about our life force energy and the shamanic technique of soul retrieval.

Katie, Byron. *Loving What Is: Four Questions That Can Change Your Life*. New York: Three Rivers Press, 2003.
—Transform the stories you are telling yourself and get closer to the truth.

Myss, Caroline. *Why People Don't Heal and How They Can*. New York: Bantam Press, 1998.

O'Donoghue, John. *Anam Cara*. New York: Bantam Press, 1997.
—A beautiful, spiritual book to help you find beauty in everyday life and connect to grace at all times.

—This book may help explain any resistance you may be having to the healing process. Lots to think about here, and her other books are also excellent.

Pierce, Penney. *Frequency*. New York: Atria, 2009.
—Getting bearings on your personal energy frequency and how to raise your vibration.

Rankin, Lissa. *Mind Over Medicine: Scientific Proof that You Can Heal Yourself*. Carlsbad, CA: Hay House, 2014.
—Written by a doctor, this book talks about how you can empower yourself as a patient. It also explains alternatives to traditional medicine.

Shinn, Florence Scovel. *The Game of Life and How to Play It*. Camarillo, CA: DeVorss & Company, 1978.
—The original book on manifestation and energy.

Tracy, Brian. *The Psychology of Achievement*. New York: Simon & Schuster, 2002.
—Mostly anything by Brian Tracy is good for goal-setting and developing a practical, positive mindset about creating a life you love.

Turner, Toko-pa. *Belonging*. Salt Spring Island, BC: Her Own Room Press, 2017.
—This rich book steps into dreamwork and shamanism, exploring the connection between us all and why some people still feel lonely.

Villodo, Alberto. *Shaman, Healer, Sage*. New York: Bantam, 2001.
—Full of ways to work with energy as well as a different perspective on life.

Virtue, Doreen. *The Lightworker's Way*. Carlsbad, CA: Hay House, 2005.
—A wonderful book with Doreen's story about her discovery of angels and healing, and how it affected her life.

Vitale, Joe. *The Awakening Course*. New York: John Wiley & Sons, 2010.
—Joe looks at energy clearing and enlightenment, becoming aware, and maximizing your potential to create a life you love.

Williamson, Marianne. *A Return to Love*. New York: HarperOne, 1996.
—The story of Marianne's journey of healing, interspersed with the philosophy of *A Course in Miracles*.

Appendix

Choosing a Therapist and Therapy That's Right for You

Asking for Help

This section is by no means complete, but throughout the book I've said "don't be afraid to ask for help," so I want to give you some understanding of what types of help exist. In my years of experience as a therapist, I've found that at times, therapists make clients feel disempowered. My aim here is to give you information that will empower you to ask good questions before you make an appointment and to know your rights when it comes to therapy so you will be able make the right decision for yourself based on your own good judgment and intuition.

Many people decide to train in a specific therapy and become a therapist instead of actually going through the process as a client and doing the work they need to do. If you do want to become a therapist, you'll become a stronger, more authentic therapist if you begin as a client and make a good start on your own work before beginning any training programs. Additionally, you'll gain the knowledge of what it's like to be a client, which will enhance your personal skills if you decide to become a therapist.

A Note on Regulating Bodies

A regulating body is a group or organization that creates rules, standards, and guidelines for correct practice. It is the place to go to find a credible professional therapist in a specialized field of work. This may sound technical, but if something goes wrong during a session, it's good to have this information from the outset.

There are two of types of regulating body: statutory regulating bodies (run by the state or government) and nonstatutory or self-regulating bodies (independent bodies that run themselves). It is usually a long and difficult process to be listed as an accredited practitioner for a state-regulated body; self-regulating bodies are much less rigorous but the standards may not be as high depending on who is running the body in question. You won't find a state-regulating body for most complementary therapies (that is, therapies that are used in conjunction with conventional medical treatments), as the state doesn't tend to get involved in holistic work; however, it does take an active interest in psychology and psychotherapy, which is why I mention it here. In the US, licenses will usually be required for any practicing psychotherapist; however, it is quite different in Europe and the rest of the world.

The advantage of looking up a regulating body for a therapist is having a comeback as a client if something goes wrong. You also have the expectation of a certain standard of practice from your therapist. If the practitioner does not adhere to the rules for correct practice, you have a right to make a complaint to the regulating body; the consequences for the therapist may include investigation leading to being removed from the register of practitioners.

If you want to find a register of practitioners for a particular therapy before choosing your therapist, you can do a web search. Types of keywords you could use could be "regulating body for reflexology in [your state]." Please note that looking up something like "register of practitioners for Reiki in London [or another large city]" could actually bring up a website where practitioners pay to be listed and aren't covered by any regulation whatsoever.

Visit the websites in your search results and make up your own mind based on the information you find there. You can also look up a register of practitioners related to a specific school or college to find former pupils, which could be a good idea if a school you know of has a good reputation. From there, you can contact the therapists and ask them the questions in the following section.

At the end of the day, a good therapy session still comes down to your confidence in your therapist and the relationship between you. The next section gives some guidelines and questions to ask any therapist in advance of scheduling a session.

Choosing a Psychotherapist

There are so many types of therapy to choose from; it can be very confusing. I've listed and categorized some of the therapies here to make it a bit easier. Note that only the more common types are listed. My descriptions aren't definitive; they are brief, to give you a taste of what each therapy is about. If something appeals to you, I urge you to look into it further to make a choice.

Counseling: Talking with someone to gain perspective on your life situation. This is non-directive—no advice is given and it is client-driven, i.e., the client chooses what to talk about. It usually takes about four to six sessions of counseling to work through an issue.

Psychotherapy: This can be more directive in that once it's clear what the client is looking to do, the therapist takes a more active role. Therapists of this type can suggest techniques and a direction to work in using different processes to help create transformation. There may be homework in the form of tasks (such as keeping a journal), so for this reason several sessions may be required.

Psychotherapy is really more about the relationship you create with the therapist than the type of therapy on offer. For that reason, you need to make an emotional connection with your therapist. Many psychotherapists use an integrative approach, which means that they are versed in several different modes of therapy and they blend them together as needed in a session. The number of sessions required for psychotherapy/counselling are usually set between you and the therapist and can be decided up front or on a session-by-session basis. Keep in mind that you have rights to negotiate this, so if a psychotherapist demands six sessions' payment up front and you ask for a trial session or to pay on a session-by-session basis and they don't waver, it's a signal to you as to how the sessions themselves may proceed. Remember, if you feel you aren't enjoying the process, connecting with the therapist, or comfortable with the work, you can end the sessions at any time.

Psychoanalysis: A very intensive therapy where the psycho-analyst studies your thought patterns and history and makes a diagnosis over many sessions. You do most of the talking. The therapist asks questions and traditionally sits behind you, so there's no eye contact. This may involve going back to trauma and childhood events, talking about dreams, and so on.

Bereavement Counseling: A specialized form of counseling that helps you move on from any kind of loss, not just the loss of a loved one in your life.

Cognitive Behavioral Therapy: This psychotherapeutic pro-cess concentrates on looking at your thought patterns and teaching you ways to change them to healthier ones.

Gestalt: A process that uses talking and feeling to work through problems. This type of therapy offers a holistic approach, working with the emotional body. It can be very powerful and at times may seem similar to the mind-fulness energy-healing exercises in this book.

Human Givens: A type of psychotherapy that works on a frame-work based on the idea that people have a set of needs that have to be met.

Transpersonal Therapy: Psychotherapy that works with a belief in God or something greater than us to help manage life situations.

Other forms of therapy may include art therapy, brief therapy, family therapy, group therapy, play therapy, positive psychology, and transactional therapy.

It's very useful to talk about the therapy process with the therapist, i.e., check in and tell them you're really benefitting from the sessions, or let them know if you're not happy. Talking about the therapy process with the therapist can dramatically improve the results, as both of you are more aware of what is going on. Sometimes it can be your resistance to the work making you unhappy with the therapy rather than anything the therapist is doing.

Group therapy is when a group of people have a session together, though the individuals aren't always at the same points in their individual work. If you take part in it, you will be exposed to other people's processes. If you're sensitive or not ready for it, you can pick up on the group energies as well as the ones you're already trying to work with, which can make things difficult for you. There are also group dynamics to keep in mind that you wouldn't get if you were in a one-on-one. Keep in mind that a one-on-one session may be what you need if you're feeling fragile.

Questions to Ask a Psychotherapist/Counselor

- How long have you been in practice?

- Are you a current member of an accrediting body? Do you have a license?

- Where did you get your degree?

- How much do you charge for your sessions?

- Do you report to anyone?

- Do I need to sign up for a certain number of sessions?

- Do you have a cancellation policy?

- Do you accept personal health insurance?

Choosing the Right Energy Therapy

When thinking about the number of energy therapies now available, it can be overwhelming to work out what you need. Please know that like psychotherapy, the success of energy healing can be more about the relationship between you and the therapist than about the therapy itself. There may be some very gifted energy healers out there who aren't qualified or certified in mainstream modalities (ways of working) and you could be missing out if you decide not to see them for that reason.

Every therapist will be different and every session will be different, but there are some commonalities. For example, when receiving energy healing there is no need for you to remove your clothing. You will typically lie down and the therapist will place their hands on or over your body, drawing down the universal life force energy into your biological energy field. These therapies can work over plaster casts if you have a broken limb; they can also work over distance if you can't make it into the therapist's office for a treatment.

Types of energy therapies include (but are not exclusive to) the following:

- bioenergy healing
- crystal healing
- EmoTrance
- Hands of Light holistic healing
- Integrated Energy Therapy (IET)
- Johrei
- Life Alignment therapy
- past-life regression
- pranic healing
- Quantum Touch
- Rahanni Celestial Healing
- Reconnection healing
- Reiki (there are many forms—Usui, Karuna, Tibetan, Angelic, Tera Mai, Rainbow, Dragon, Kundalini—all of which have different methods to access the universal life force energy)
- Restorative Touch
- Sakura
- Seichem
- ThetaHealing

You can research each type of healing if you wish to know more about it. I also suggest looking for a recommendation from someone who has been to the healer you are considering. Remember, this is more about the healer than about the modality of healing; some people are born to be healers and may not even have trained formally, so they may simply offer you "spiritual healing." Others who have trained for years may not be natural healers but may do a great job helping you release energies and acting as a witness for you. You will only know if you try.

Many therapists tend to mix several therapies together and don't usually tell the client in advance, so ask when booking if it's pure Reiki, for example, or if they combine it with something else.

Remember that everyone is different and training is different too. For example, each Reiki master will teach in their own way, so Reiki students will all receive different training. When looking for a therapist, do your homework first: look at their website, read their blog, and get a feel for their energy. Nowadays, there is online training available for energy healers, and you can complete a master's program over a very short period of time. Note that this doesn't make you a master therapist, but some people call themselves such regardless. You need to be sure that you are going to a well-practiced professional. It's useful to ask some or all of the following questions.

Questions to Ask an Energy Therapist

- How long have you been providing energy-healing treatments?
- How much do you charge for a session?
- What level of training do you have?

- Where did you train? Was your training in person with a teacher in a hands-on setting or online?
- When did you complete your training?
- How many client hours have you completed?
- Have you got full public liability insurance?
- Can I contact one of your clients for a reference?
- What should I expect in a session?
- Do you practice healing on yourself every day?

If the therapist gets standoffish, worried, or upset with you for asking these questions, they might not be the right person for you. The last question, about self-healing and self-care, is very important—as a therapist they will be seeing many people, and if they don't look after themselves and clear/raise their own vibrations, they may be passing their clients' energy over to you, and you don't want that.

Psychic readings are not part of an energy healing session. After the session, if the therapist has information for you based on what they have read in your energies, treat it as information that is true for that therapist at that moment. Nothing has to be set in stone. Everything can change. Sometimes additional information from a therapist is useful, such as them letting you know that you're not really grounded in your body. They might tell you to spend some time focusing on that issue to feel better.

When it comes to energy healing, take care to not deeply embrace everything you hear. Only pay attention with what resonates with you. As you do your work, you'll become more clear on what your work is, and you'll be more empowered to decide for yourself what you need to do.

Therapies That Combine Talking and Energy Healing

The following therapies combine talking with energetic healing. Again, there are probably many more therapies in existence than listed here.

Emotional Freedom Technique (EFT): Uses tapping on energy points and affirmations in a set framework to shift energy and work with thought patterns.

Energy Coaching: There are many coaches out there offering energy work; be aware, however, that coaching isn't always therapeutic. (Imagine a coach on a running field shouting at an athlete!) Coaching can help you set goals and become more confident, whereas therapy is something I believe should be loving, gentle, and transformational.

Hypnotherapy: The therapist goes into your subconscious mind and inserts a script or a program to change behavior or transform an irrational fear. It can involve energy work or not, depending on the therapist.

Shamanism: Shamanic methods vary dramatically, depending on the training and background of the practitioner. You really need to investigate the therapist before you book a shamanic healing session. Do find out where they trained and how long they have been in practice. Consider getting a recommendation before booking, as this therapy really does depend on the individual practitioner.

Therapies That Work with the Body

Even though they are focused directly on the physical body, bodywork therapies can really help release blocked emotions and are a great complement to any energy work or psychotherapeutic work you may be doing.

Massage: There are many different types of massage, depending on how deep and strong a treatment you wish to receive. You have a right to know if the massage therapist incorporates energy healing with the massage: sometimes practitioners close the session with Reiki because it's nice, but that might not be what you expected. You can tell them to stop if you're unhappy with it.

Reflexology: Using pressure points on the feet to heal the whole body energetically.

Reiki Massage: The therapist combines Reiki with physical massage.

Rolfing/Myofascial Release: Releasing energies within the connecting tissues in the body.

Shiatsu: A type of massage where the therapist can release trapped energies from the muscles as well as work with the physical muscles in the body.

The questions to ask before booking a bodywork treatment are similar to the ones already listed above.

Combining Bodywork with Energy Healing

You can incorporate energy healing into body movements to create a strong, grounding practice that will keep you healthy.

Healing may not always be the intention behind a bodywork class, but sometimes you'll find it sneaks its way in regardless. Make sure the facilitator is experienced and you feel safe within the group. Try a walk-in class before you sign up for a whole term. This type of practice is more about maintenance of a good energetic state than a portal into deep transformational work. However, people have been known to experience deep healing during this type of work, even though it's not necessarily the intention behind the class.

- Biodanza

- Chakra dancing

- Qigong

- Seven Rhythms dancing

- Tai chi

- Yoga—There are many traditional forms of yoga such as Astanga, Hatha, Kundalini, Raja, and so on as well as many new nontraditional forms such as antigravity, Bikram, Iyengar, and Laughter, to name a few.

Therapies for the Environment

You might find after doing energy work that you want to change the energies in your house or in your place of work.

Feng Shui: The practitioner will come and survey your building and give recommendations on where to put particular types of furniture, what colors to use, and how to position items for the optimum energy flow.

House/Land Clearing: There are land healers who are sha-
mans. They can come to your house/workplace and work
directly with energy blocks in the land. If the energy is
being disrupted by a power line, they can help you work
around it to improve the general energy flow in the space.

To Write the Author

If you wish to contact the author or would like more information about this book, please write to the author in care of Llewellyn Worldwide, and we will forward your request. Both the author and publisher appreciate hearing from you and learning of your enjoyment of this book and how it has helped you. Llewellyn Worldwide cannot guarantee that every letter written to the author can be answered, but all will be forwarded. Please write to:

Abby Wynne
℅ Llewellyn Worldwide
2143 Wooddale Drive
Woodbury, MN 55125.2989

Please enclose a self-addressed stamped envelope for reply, or $1.00 to cover costs. If outside the U.S.A., enclose an international postal reply coupon.

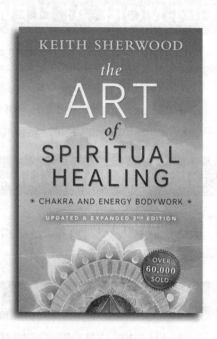

The Art of Spiritual Healing
Chakra and Energy Bodywork
Keith Sherwood

Uncover new ways to connect with the incredible healing energy that is always flowing through you in this second edition of Keith Sherwood's bestselling book. Expanding the scope beyond physical disease, *The Art of Spiritual Healing* now has chapters on healing energetic traumas and relationships, as well as maintaining wellness in a complex and stressful world. Many original healing techniques have also been streamlined and simplified, making it easier to enrich your body, soul, and spirit.

Featuring new illustrations, new mudra practices, and step-by-step directions to new and classic techniques, this handbook helps you build and maintain good health.

978-0-7387-4660-9, 288 pp., 6 x 9   **$17.99**

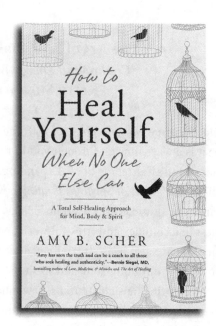

How to
Heal
Yourself
*When No One
Else Can*

A Total Self-Healing Approach
for Mind, Body & Spirit

AMY B. SCHER

"Amy has seen the truth and can be a coach to all those
who seek healing and authenticity."--**Bernie Siegel, MD,**
bestselling author of *Love, Medicine, & Miracles* and *The Art of Healing*

How to Heal Yourself from Anxiety When No One Else Can
AMY B. SCHER

This exceptional book is a unique, go-at-your-own-pace approach full of hands-on techniques and guidance that illustrate one profound truth: healing from anxiety *is* possible. Join Amy B. Scher—author of the bestselling *How to Heal Yourself When No One Else Can*—as she shares her proven methods for healing the roots of anxiety by changing harmful beliefs, calming your body, and releasing old emotional energy that holds you back.

This book guides you through a series of transformative tools and easy-to-follow exercises that can change your life quickly. No more struggling—you *can* heal. Utilizing Amy's powerful self-created techniques, as well as her own version of tapping and the widely popular Emotional Freedom Technique (EFT), you will learn how to let go of unresolved emotional baggage so that you can become the healthiest, most relaxed and lighthearted version of yourself.

978-0-7387-5646-2, 288 pp., 5.25 x 8   **$17.99**

THE HEALER'S MANUAL

*A Beginner's Guide to Energy Healing
for Yourself and Others*

TED ANDREWS

The Healer's Manual
A Beginner's Guide to Energy Healing for Yourself and Others
TED ANDREWS

Noted healer and author Ted Andrews reveals how unbalanced or blocked emotions, attitudes, and thoughts deplete our natural physical energies and make us more susceptible to illness. *The Healer's Manual* shows specific techniques—involving color, sound, fragrance, herbs, and gemstones—to restore the natural flow of energy. Use the simple practices in this book to activate healing, alleviate aches and pains, and become the healthy person you're meant to be.

978-0-87542-007-3, 264 pp., 6 x 9   **$16.99**